Quick & Easy
SKETCHES
for Scrapbookers

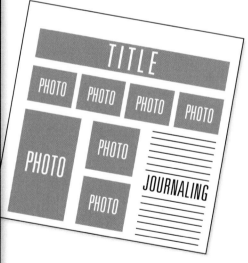

MEMORY MAKERS BOOKS

Jump-Start Your Page Design With These Timesaving Templates

Managing Editor MaryJo Regier

Art Director Nick Nyffeler

Designers Jordan Kinney, Robin Rozum

Art Acquisitions Editor Janetta Abucejo Wieneke

Craft Editor Jodi Amidei

Photographer Ken Trujillo

Contributing Photographers Lizzy Creazzo, Jennifer Reeves

Writer Nicole Cummings

Editorial Support Karen Cain, Amy Glander, Emily Curry Hitchingham, Dena Twinem

Contributing Memory Makers Masters Jessie Baldwin, Valerie Barton, Joanna Bolick, Jennifer Bourgeault, Jenn Brookover, Susan Cyrus, Lisa Dixon, Sheila Doherty, Kathy Fesmire, Diana Graham, Angie Head, Jodi Heinen, Jeniece Higgins, Nicola Howard, Diana Hudson, Julie Johnson, Kelli Noto, Heidi Schueller, Torrey Scott, Trudy Sigurdson, Shannon Taylor, Denise Tucker, Andrea Lyn Vetten-Marley, Samantha Walker, Holle Wiktorek

Memory Makers® Quick and Easy Sketches For Scrapbookers
Copyright © 2005 Memory Makers Books
All rights reserved.

Published by Memory Makers Books, an imprint of F+W Publications, Inc.
12365 Huron Street, Suite 500, Denver, CO 80234
Phone 1-800-254-9124

First edition. Printed in the United States of America.

09 08 07 06 05   5 4 3 2 1

Library of Congress Cataloging-in-Publication Data

Quick & easy sketches for scrapbookers : jump-start your page design with these
time saving templates.-- 1st ed.
    p. cm
Includes index.
ISBN 1-892127-64-4
1. Photograph albums. 2. Scrapbooks.

TR501.Q53 2005
745.593--dc22

2005052217

Distributed to trade and art markets by
F+W Publications, Inc.
4700 East Galbraith Road, Cincinnati, OH 45236
Phone (800) 289-0963
ISBN 1-892127-64-4

Distributed in Canada by Fraser Direct
100 Armstrong Avenue
Georgetown, ON, Canada L7G 5S4
Tel: (905) 877-4411

Distributed in the U.K. and Europe by David & Charles
Brunel House, Newton Abbot, Devon, TQ12 4PU, England
Tel: (+44) 1626 323200, Fax: (+44) 1626 323319
E-mail: mail@davidandcharles.co.uk

Distributed in Australia by Capricorn Link
P.O. Box 704, S. Windsor NSW, 2756 Australia
Tel: (02) 4577-3555

Memory Makers Books is the home of *Memory Makers*, the scrapbook magazine dedicated to educating and inspiring scrapbookers. To subscribe, or for more information, call 1-800-366-6465.
Visit us on the Internet at www.memorymakersmagazine.com.

This book belongs to:

_____

We dedicate this book to all of our *Memory Makers*
readers who strive to find more time for scrapbooking,
and to the featured artists herein who skillfully and
cleverly brought our sketches to life.

Introduction

Our busy lives constantly call for ways to save time and scrapbook faster. One of the best and most inexpensive ways to get a lot of scrapbook pages completed quickly is by using formula page sketches that are easily adaptable to any page theme. Sketches eliminate the guesswork of page design by supplying you with a plan for the placement of scrapbooking's most crucial page elements—your photos, page title and journaling. As such, these highly versatile sketches provide a foolproof foundation for quick-and-easy page design, allowing you to focus more energy on the creative aspect of scrapbooking!

This book contains 33 reproducible master sketches that can be rotated four ways, and then flipped (mirror image) and rotated four ways again, for a grand total of 264 sketches that can be used over and over again. By simply rotating or altering a sketch idea or changing the page theme, colors and page accents, one sketch can be used to create endless varieties of scrapbook pages in short order—with a fresh and unique look each time.

For quick-and-easy reference, our sketches are organized by chapters based on the number of photos on the sketch—from single-photo pages to pages with multiple photos in a variety of sizes. Each sketch is also shown in use three different ways: in a simple yet stunning layout, a graphic layout and an enhanced layout—all of which are useful to you, the reader, for selecting a sketch and layout idea that suits your time and scrapbook skill level best.

You'll also discover how to get the most from this book, how to convert sketches for different-sized layouts, how to create two-page spreads from one sketch, how to make your own sketches, where to find sources for sketch inspiration and how to keep your sketches organized for quick reference. Even if you have never scrapbooked using sketches before, you must try it! You will find their ease of use both efficient and creatively liberating!

MaryJo

MaryJo Regier, Managing Editor
Memory Makers Books

Simple—Designed to be uncomplicated and easy pages that offer simplified ways to create stunning layouts in less than one hour.

Graphic—Linear, crisp and illustrative techniques for using the principals and concepts of graphically-inspired design on scrapbook pages.

Enhanced—Showcasing innovative techniques and elaborate designs produced to stimulate even the advanced scrapbooker.

TABLE OF CONTENTS

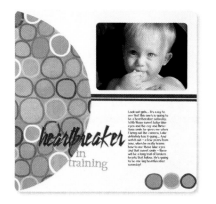

Getting the Most From This Book

The quick-and-easy sketches in this book serve as a useful tool for you to complete any type of layout swiftly and uniquely. Each sketch is designed to be used with any skill level of scrapbooking and can be altered to fit your needs and/or artistic desires. Sketches can be used in their simplest form by following the sketch exactly or by merely changing one, two, or more of the elements of the sketch for a layout that is unique to you. This flexibility is what makes working with sketches one of the most efficient ways to quickly and easily create your greatest layouts.

Using sketches at the designing stage of a layout is not only a great timesaver, but an easy way to get a jump-start on your pages. Which styles or techniques you use is completely up to you, the artist. Here are some tips and ideas to get you going:

Sketches can be flipped to create a mirror image or rotated, like the sketch below was, to create a well-balanced, two-page spread.

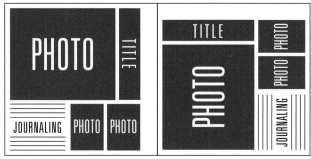

CONVERTING SKETCHES FOR DIFFERENT-SIZED LAYOUTS

Sketches are drawn up in either 12 x 12" or 8½ x 11" formats and can be changed to accommodate either size. To translate a 12 x 12" sketch into an 8½ x 11" layout, downsize elements on the page. For example, use smaller photos, smaller journaling box and fewer page accents. Likewise, converting an 8½ x 11" sketch into a 12 x 12" is as easy as making the elements larger and using more accents. Sketches help produce well-balanced layouts in any format; therefore, you cannot go wrong with whichever sketch size you choose.

CREATING TWO-PAGE SPREADS FROM ONE SKETCH

For two-page spreads, sketches can be flipped to create a mirror image. For variation, sketches can also be turned upside down, turned 90 degrees, 180 degrees, and so on to get a different look every time. The possibilities of using sketches are endless and are not limited to the number of photos you have or to a page theme.

HOW THIS BOOK IS STRUCTURED

Use of this book has been completely simplified for you, the reader. It will serve as a valuable tool to get your creative juices flowing. Do you have just one great photo to scrapbook? Chapter one is dedicated to single-photo sketches. Have more than one photo? More than four? Each chapter is structured around the number of photos used in the sketch. In this book you are shown three examples of how each sketch was used. One example shows a graphic/linear design while another shows an easy/simple design, and the third example shows an advanced/enhanced design—giving you the ability to "see" the sketch in any way that suits your artistic abilities, needs and desires.

WHAT YOU NEED TO GET STARTED

By now, you probably cannot wait to get started in creating layouts from sketches but may be asking yourself, "What do I need to do to get started?" It is simple! Gather up your photos and pick a sketch. Lay out your photos according to the sketch and make notes of any changes you want to make. Then, with your sketch and notes in hand, choose your papers, page embellishments, and any accents you wish to use. When done, use your sketch to help you quickly and easily create your layout.

Making Your Own Sketches

Have you ever thought of a layout idea while in the middle of something and quickly sketched it out? Or maybe you have considered sketching but thought you wouldn't know how to do it? You might even be asking, "What will sketching do for me?" Sketching is not only a great way to mentally prepare for your layout, but also a great way to rough draft the page before you actually commit it to layout form. Sketching will also help you develop your own personal style. Once you start sketching your layouts on a regular basis, you might begin to notice a reccurring pattern in your pages—a pattern that shows your own unique style. There are no rules to sketching, and once you start you might find that it will take you down creative avenues you've never traveled before!

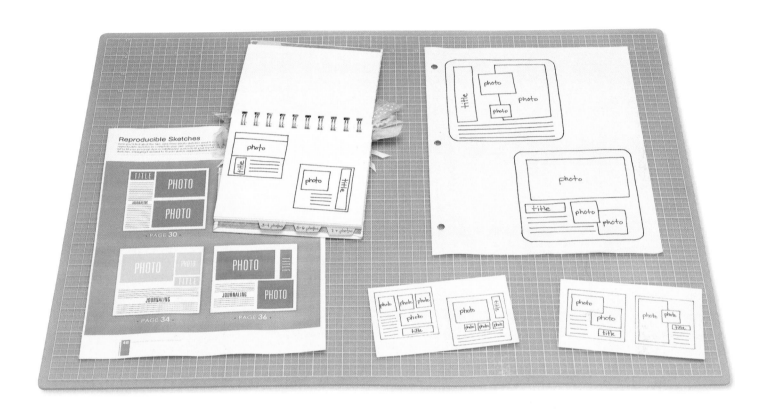

HAND-DRAWN SKETCHES

Hand-drawn sketches are probably the easiest to do because they can be done whenever and wherever the inspiration strikes you. Sketch pads are abundant as are the variations of them. Have a few different sizes on hand. Use a larger sized book when sketching at home or at a crop. A smaller, pocket- or purse-size sketch pad works well for traveling or when you are out and about and get an idea.

COMPUTER SKETCHES

Is creating sketches on the computer, using text boxes, more your cup of tea? Using software or programs such as Digital Image Pro, Paint Shop, and even Microsoft Word or Microsoft PowerPoint to create sketches can be a quick and easy way of moving elements around on a blank canvas to achieve maximum results. Simply print the sketches out to follow along or use them when creating your digital layouts.

PREMADE OR PHOTOCOPIED SKETCHES

Premade sketches such as the ones found at the end of each chapter of this book can be used to jump-start your own self-made sketches. Photocopy them and make notes of changes you would like to make to create a newer, updated version of one you may have already used or have previous plans for.

Finding Sources for Sketch Inspiration

Sources for new sketches are everywhere you turn and are probably in places you haven't even thought of. They are like new discoveries waiting to be unearthed. Look around your current surroundings. What do you see? Maybe it is the way your paintings are arranged on a wall with other miscellaneous décor. Or maybe it is a particular painting itself that catches your eye. If you were to sketch out these elements of design, could this become a rough draft for a layout? Most likely, the answer is yes. Try applying the same designer's eye in any environment you are in. Take note of the design of the outside of a building or structure, for example, or of a sign or billboard. You will be surprised to see that once you train your mind to look for inspiration, your sources for sketching will become plentiful. Here are a few more ideas to help get you going:

SCRAPBOOK MAGAZINES AND IDEA BOOKS

Completed layouts that are featured in scrapbooking magazines or idea books are a great source of inspiration. Reproduce a layout in a quick sketch to have on hand for the next time you sit down to scrapbook. The hard work of having to come up with your design is already done for you!

OTHER MAGAZINES AND BOOKS

Look to other magazines and craft and graphic-design books for ideas. Don't make the mistake of thinking it has to be scrapbook-related to sketch it. Next time you are in your craft store, browse some of the non-scrapbooking craft books and use your portable sketchpad to take some notes or jot down any sketch ideas that inspire you. If something catches your eye—whether an abstract graphic, a pretty element, an article you are reading or an advertisement you see—think about what you could pull from it to use on a page.

GREETING CARDS

Another source for sketches you will find inspirational is greeting cards. Examine a card that appeals to you. How is the card laid out? Is this design something that can move onto a larger canvas? How about where the text is placed? Will this work for a title or journaling? With little to no tweaking, using a greeting card to stimulate your creativity will lead to some very productive sketches.

THE INTERNET

Web pages are especially beneficial for sketching stimulation. Think about the people behind the design. Professional Web designers brainstorm these sites and specialize in graphic design. What better inspiration? Use everything from their color combinations to the way their page elements are laid out for fail-proof sketches.

Keeping Sketches Organized

Once you start sketching you will find that like all of your scrapbooking supplies and materials, you will need an effective way to store and organize your sketches. When developing your organizational strategy, you will want to keep a few things in mind. First, you will want to have quick-and-easy access to the sketches so that when you need them for inspiration or reference, they won't be hard to find. Next, organize them in a way that makes sense for you. Perhaps the simplest way to file sketches for quick reference is to organize them by the number of photos used on the sketches. Look below for more helpful suggestions and tips on storing your sketches.

LARGER SKETCHES

The size of storage you choose depends on the size of sketches you are organizing. If you are using larger sheets of paper, you have a few options. One way to organize and store them is in sheet protectors and then in a binder. Separate sketches in the binder with tabbed dividers organized by number of photos, by theme or by events. Slip your binder into your cropping supplies to take with you on crops. File folders also work well for larger sketches and are easily organized since they are already divided. This solution becomes even more resourceful when you store papers and elements you plan on using for the layouts inside the same slots where you store the sketches.

SMALLER SKETCHES

If you are using smaller sketches such as recipe cards or index cards, the easiest storage solution is in a recipe card file or index box sorted with tabbed dividers. Maybe the thought of smaller storage appeals to you but you have sketches in larger formats? The easy solution here is to scan the sketches into your computer or photocopy them, reduce in size and print them out. You can also cut sketches out and adhere them onto index or recipe cards.

NUMBERING SYSTEM ALTERNATIVE

A super-organized tip for the super-organized scrapbooker that will make use of your sketches even more proficient, is to assign a number to each sketch that is filed or stored. Whether it is a hand-drawn sketch, a reproduced sketch, or photocopied sketch, number them consecutively each time you store or file them. Keep an index of where each numbered sketch is stored. Then, when you find a sketch that will work perfectly for specific photos, write the sketch number down on a calendar on a day you know you will be working on those photos. This will save time and make getting started that much quicker and easier.

Single-Photo
SKETCHES

chapter one

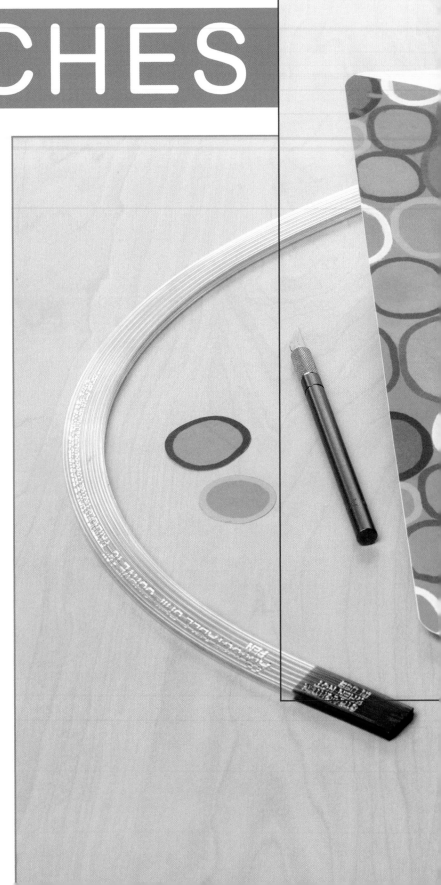

As you flip through the latest batch of photos you have developed or printed, you find a single photo that captures your attention unlike any of the others. Maybe it is one of several photos you took at a particular event or a particular place, or maybe it is just a single snapshot. Regardless, it is a photo that evokes strong enough emotion that you want to showcase it alone on a layout.

If you have never tried a single-photo layout, or even if you are a veteran at it, single-photo sketches can be a very useful tool in getting your layout to come out as perfect as the photo you are displaying. Single-photo sketches are a blueprint for all of the important elements on a page and are open for any type of artistic interpretation, alteration or additions. As you will see inside this chapter, the sketches can be applied in their literal or graphic form, or can be altered with simple or advanced techniques.

The photo can be enlarged to cover the entire page or the majority of the page, giving foremost emphasis to it. You can also alter the photo into a fun shape or layer embellishments and accents on it for visual interest. Whatever your artistic style is, these sketches provide a quick and easy way to get appealing single-photo layouts.

heartbreaker
in training

Look out girls... It's easy to see that this one's is going to be a heartbreaker someday. With those sweet baby blue eyes and the coy and flirtatious smile he gives me when I bring out the camera, Luke definitely has it going... And watch out – a few years from now, when he really learns how to use those blue eyes and that sweet smile – there will be a long trail of broken hearts that follow. He's going to be one big heartbreaker someday!

PHOTO

TITLE

JOURNALING

Graphic

Jennifer personalizes the sketch to bring equal attention to the photo and journaling. Large and small circles are added for graphic appeal. She then adds strips to the larger circle creating a sun on which to situate her title, effectively tying the title, photo and journaling all together.

SUNSHINE
Jennifer Bourgeault, Macomb Township, Michigan

Supplies: Patterned papers (Chatterbox, Junkitz); letter stickers (Colorbök); cardstock; circle cutter; button

sunshine

Connor, I know it sounds kinda cliché...but you truly are my sunshine! No matter how my day is going, or how frustrated I may be, you always seem to know how to put a great big smile on my face. The funny thing is, you can even manage to do this when YOU are the source of my frustration (yes, baby, there are times that even sweet little you can frustrate someone!) You just have such a precious demeanor about you, from the way you look to your sweet little voice. It just melts my heart thinking about all the sweet things you say to me. "Mama, you're beautiful." "You're sweet, Mama." "I love you the best." You certainly got a gift and there is no doubt about it ~ you know how to use it! Yep, you're my sunshine, kiddo! Photo taken September 2004

Simple

Jenn enlarges her photo to fit the full length of her page, as opposed to the smaller one on the sketch, making it the main emphasis of the layout. To ground the paper and embellishments, she provides continuity by expanding the red line in the photo with red ribbon.

LOOK MOMMY I'M MAGIC
Jenn Brookover, San Antonio, Texas

Supplies: Patterned papers (7 Gypsies, Li'l Davis Designs, Magenta, Scenic Route Paper Co.); wooden letters (Westrim); wish tag (Melissa Frances); letter stamps (FontWerks); ribbons (Li'l Davis Designs, May Arts); rickrack (Offray); stamping ink; transparency

What would a trip to St. Louis be without a visit to the Magic House? Complete with huge slides, a whole room of sand, and all kinds of fun games, it truly is a child's paradise. After tackling all of these areas, we finally came upon the water room. Filled with water guns, a huge running waterway and a lot of wet kids, our final stop was the bubble maker. Jake jumped right in and pulled the rope up...like he'd done it a million times before. As I reached for my camera, he yelled out "Look Mommy, I'm MAGIC"! What a great way to end the day!

Enhanced

Julie utilizes this sketch to draw your eye to the photo by surrounding it with many elements that enhance it. To soften the boldness of the sketch, she uses a large circle cut from patterned paper, bringing your eye around again to her photo. A complementary-colored piece of fabric is cut to use for an attractive title.

TAKING A MOMENT
Julie Johnson, Seabrook, Texas

Supplies: Patterned paper (7 Gypsies); textured cardstock (Prism Papers); metal embellishments (Go West Studios, Making Memories, Nunn Design); printed ribbon (Making Memories); synonym tab (Autumn Leaves); brads; stamping ink; transparency; fabric

taking a moment...
from your busy day. a dozen kids to play with, acres to run in. i find you sitting under the oak tree. taking it all in. wondering how this tree got so tall. just a simple question that deserves a simple answer...

"a million moments just like these."

Graphic

This sketch's theory allowed Danielle to fashion a unique title for her page. A label holder, added as part of the title, provides a directional element pointing your eye toward the journaling. She places rub-on letters and a charming quote atop the photo for visual interest.

SLIDING AT THE ATLANTA ZOO
Danielle Thompson, Tucker, Georgia

Supplies: Patterned papers (Karen Foster Design); letter stickers (Paper Loft); quote sticker (Cloud 9 Design); label holder (7 Gypsies); "Z" tab (Autumn Leaves); rub-on letters (Creative Imaginations); cardstock; ribbon; rickrack; transparency

Simple

Kimberly balances her oversized photo with a charming, acrylic polka-dot frame to enhance her title area based on the sketch. The photo is mounted off-center atop a stitched mat, and a stitched photo corner is added for an accent. To tie in her title with the rest of her layout, she alters the sketch with a section of polka-dot patterned paper mounted down the left side of her page, making the page whimsical and fun.

LOVE

Kimberly Kesti, Phoenix, Arizona

Supplies: Patterned papers, acrylic frame (Making Memories); textured cardstock (Bazzill); letter stickers (KI Memories); die-cut flower (Accu-Cut); rub-on quote (K & Company); twill tape (Creek Bank Creations); staples

Enhanced

For distinction, Heather uses creative circles for her journaling accented with attractive silk flowers. Overlapping her journaling circles onto her photo directs your eye toward it. Balance is achieved with a full-length photo stretched across the bottom of the page as opposed to a smaller one as in the sketch. The title is accented with color-coordinating ribbons, letter buttons and a flower to complete the page.

MY SWEET GIRL

Heather Preckel, Swannanoa, North Carolina

Supplies: Patterned paper (My Mind's Eye); letter buttons (Junkitz); decorative brads (Making Memories); stencil (Autumn Leaves); ribbons (May Arts, Michaels); silk flowers; brads; stamping ink

Graphic

Jessie is able to create a visual triangle based on the concept of this sketch. Her graphic design is softened with a gingham ribbon, giving her layout more of a homespun feel. The title is enhanced with embossing powder and mounted overlapping the photo to give the feeling of cohesiveness.

MY BABY YOU'LL BE

Jessie Baldwin, Las Vegas, Nevada

Supplies: Textured cardstock (Bazzill); stencil letters (Making Memories); letter stickers (Creative Imaginations); ribbon (Offray); stamping ink; embossing powder

PHOTO

TITLE

JOURNALING

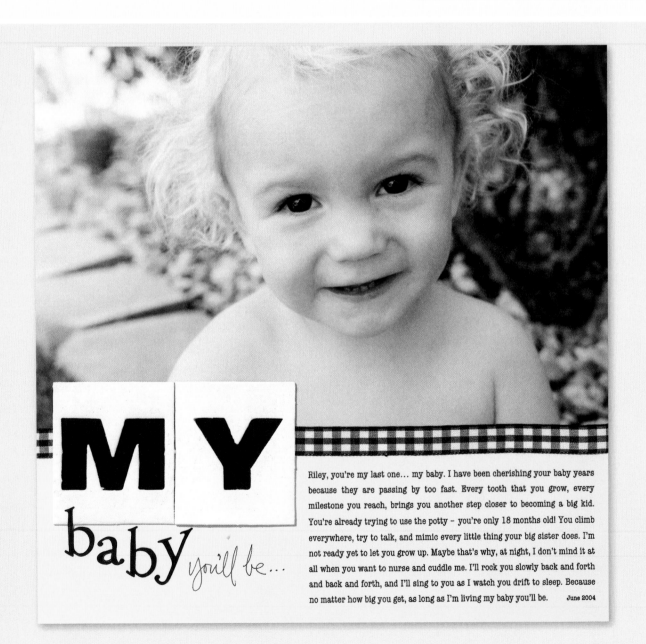

MY baby *you'll be...*

Riley, you're my last one... my baby. I have been cherishing your baby years because they are passing by too fast. Every tooth that you grow, every milestone you reach, brings you another step closer to becoming a big kid. You're already trying to use the potty – you're only 18 months old! You climb everywhere, try to talk, and mimic every little thing your big sister does. I'm not ready yet to let you grow up. Maybe that's why, at night, I don't mind it at all when you want to nurse and cuddle me. I'll rock you slowly back and forth and back and forth, and I'll sing to you as I watch you drift to sleep. Because no matter how big you get, as long as I'm living my baby you'll be.   **June 2004**

Simple

Elizabeth varies the sketch slightly by reducing the photo size, allowing her to create a delightful oversized stitched fabric mat and accents. The title and journaling placement on the sketch are followed on the layout with her re-emphasizing her title inside her journaling.

BEST SCRAPPING FRIENDS
Elizabeth Cuzzacrea, Lockport, New York

Supplies: Textured cardstocks (Bazzill, KI Memories); rub-on letters (KI Memories, Making Memories); fabrics; acrylic paint

Enhanced

Kelli uses this sketch concept to add a hand-made transparency floral frame around the photo for enhancement. To tie in the title, some of the flower accents are mounted below. A striped ribbon adds a final touch to her charming layout.

JOIE DE VIVRE!
Kelli Noto, Centennial, Colorado

Supplies: Textured cardstock (Bazzill); die-cut letters (QuicKutz); permanent marker (Sanford Corp.); stamping ink; transparency; acrylic paint; ribbon

PHOTO
TITLE
JOURNALING

Graphic

Susan follows the sketch photo placement, enhancing it with a fun curved cut to imply motion. The large space allowed on the sketch for the title and journaling gave her the ability to tie both in together, emphasizing the title words by enlarging them.

HOW DO YOU LIKE TO GO UP IN A SWING?
Susan Cyrus, Broken Arrow, Oklahoma

Supplies: Textured cardstocks (Bazzill); metal-rimmed tag (2DYE4); brads (Boxer Scrapbook Productions, Making Memories); ribbon; cardstock

How do you like to go up in a
swing
Up in the air so
blue?
Oh, I do think it the pleasantest
thing
Ever a child can do!

Robert Louis Stevenson

Having no neck, plus three chins to stabilize your head, has its advantages. Connor was able to swing higher, earlier than other babies. He loved every minute of our trips to the park!

SPRING 2002

Simple

Becky felt this sketch commanded attention to her photo so she accentuated it with a simple and earthy frame. The title is not contained in a block but rather flows into the journaling which is done in bullet style with brads. She uses brown ink to highlight all of the elements of the sketch and complete her page.

SNIPS, SNAILS & PUPPY DOG TAILS
Becky Kent, Hilliard, Ohio

Supplies: Patterned papers (Chatterbox, Pebbles); stickers, metal charm (Pebbles); die-cut letters (Sizzix); ribbon (May Arts); stamping ink; brads

Enhanced

Based on this sketch's photo placement, Lisa is able to use a dramatic photo, accenting it with ribbon, embossed Celtic cross and coordinating buttons. The journaling and title placement are kept the same but are layered with the cross accent, tying all the elements together to produce a stunning end result.

IRELAND
Lisa Dixon, East Brunswick, New Jersey
Photo: Kathy Hammesfahr, Brick, New Jersey

Supplies: Patterned vellum (Club Scrap); textured cardstocks (Bazzill, DMD); mica (USArtQuest); extra thick embossing powder (Suze Weinberg); wooden letters (Westrim); ribbon (May Arts); vellum; stamping ink; acrylic paint; decorative buttons; handkerchief scrap

Destination

c a m p
Gresham

When Daizy was younger, she used to love to ride in the boat. She had great balance and would stand at the front of the boat or sit on one of the chairs. It was her dog imitation of Leo DiCaprio in "Titanic". She was the "top dog" of the world!

Graphic

Heidi uses minimal journaling in order to maximize the space designated on the sketch for her enlarged photo. For pleasing movement on the page, her title flows into her photo. A ribbon and buckle charm are added to the bottom of the page to balance out the enlarged photo.

DESTINATION
Heidi Schueller, Waukesha, Wisconsin

Supplies: Patterned papers (Chatterbox); letter stickers (Kopp Design); rub-on word (C-Thru Ruler); buckle charm (KI Memories); mini brads (Making Memories); ribbon (Michaels); cardstock

It's a summer evening and we are out taking pics of Abby for her 1-year photo shoot. We place Abby in the garden in the flowers and you jump in there to have your pic taken with her. You adore your sister and I'd love to have a photo with you both in there but why is it that 6 year olds have such a forced smile? We don't really get a good picture of you during the photo shoot.

I finish off with Abby and start off to go inside. Just as I am about to walk in the door I see you sitting on the chair below me. I point the camera and click real quick. There it is! That gorgeous 6-year-old smile!

Dude... you are sooo cool.

Simple

To make this layout quickly but unique to her, Nic followed the sketch's placement of journaling and title but slightly enlarged her charming photo. Title and journaling are placed on contrasting backgrounds to give each its own style. To finish the layout, she adds decorative ribbon on the bottom of the page.

DUDE, YOU ARE SO COOL
Nic Howard, Pukekone, South Auckland, New Zealand

Supplies: Patterned papers (Creative Imaginations, Karen Foster Design); letter stickers (Mustard Moon); rub-on letters (Making Memories); stamping ink

Enhanced

Shannon increases the size of her photo, making it slightly larger than what the sketch calls for, giving her the impact she was looking for. To enhance the sketch, she uses strips of polka-dot and black velvet ribbon embellished with metal charms. To add depth, she uses transparency overlays on her patterned paper background.

HUNGRY BABY
Shannon Taylor, Bristol, Tennessee

Supplies: Patterned papers (Junkitz); transparency overlay, transparency frame (Creative Imaginations); metal words and charms (Making Memories); dimensional adhesive (JudiKins); ribbon (Offray, Rusty Pickle); cardstock

I'd forgotten how quick hunger can overtake a newborn. My brand new nephew Elijah reminded me how in one rumble of a belly a baby could go from a deep slumber to an award-winning scream without even opening his eyes.
Age - 2 weeks

Graphic

April takes advantage of the single-photo sketch by enlarging the photo slightly and placing it on a background of layers and textures on this computer-generated layout. To vary the title, she places it off-center on the page. The journaling is extended to the full length of the title bar for balance.

ALL BY YOURSELF
April Anderton, Springville, Utah

Supplies: Image-editing software (Photoshop CS); digital backgrounds (www.digitalscrapbooking.com)

Simple

Janetta takes a simple sketch and enhances it with accents placed on the photo, title and journaling to make it reflect her style. The title bar is expanded to make room for a larger title and cut from coordinating colors based on the patterned paper background. Journaling placement follows the sketch but is enhanced with alphabet beads.

SMILE PRETTY FOR THE CAMERA GIA

Janetta Abucejo Wieneke,
Memory Makers Books

Supplies: Patterned papers (Doodlebug Design); textured cardstocks (Bazzill); metal-rimmed tag (Avery); mini bottle cap (Li'l Davis Designs); die-cut photo corners (Sizzix); alphabet beads (Crafts, Etc.); number stickers (Making Memories); square and circle punch (EK Success); chalk ink (Clearsnap); cardstock; wire ribbon; brads

Enhanced

Suzy takes advantage of the title area on the sketch to create unique flip cards that open to show a photo and story timeline. Metal and floral accents enhance the title. For emphasis on the photo, it is enlarged and stretched across the page and accented with pretty flowers. She uses striped patterned paper on the top and bottom of her layout for balance.

IN THE BLINK OF AN EYE

Suzy West, Fremont, California

Supplies: Patterned papers (DieCuts with a View); rub-on words (Imagination Project); metal words, foam letter stamps, heart brads (Making Memories); extra thick embossing powder (Suze Weinberg); silk flowers; transparency; acrylic paint

Graphic

Samantha creates a digital layout based on this sketch, altering it to showcase her son's photo perfectly. The title is overlapped onto the main photo, soaking up some of the negative space. The journaling box incorporates the title that varies from the sketch, working nicely to balance the layout.

WAKING UP
Samantha Walker, Battle Ground, Washington

Supplies: Image-editing software (Adobe Photoshop 7.0)

After being put down for a nap in a cozy bed back at the cabin, then transported in the car to the lake while still sleeping, it is no wonder why you woke up in such a bewildered state. This picture even shows where your hand, that you were sleeping on, left an impression on your face. It must be strange and confusing to a child to drift off to sleep in one place only to wake up in a completely different environment. Their world is constantly changing over which they have no controll. They are pretty amazing little people for being able adapt quickly to new situations.

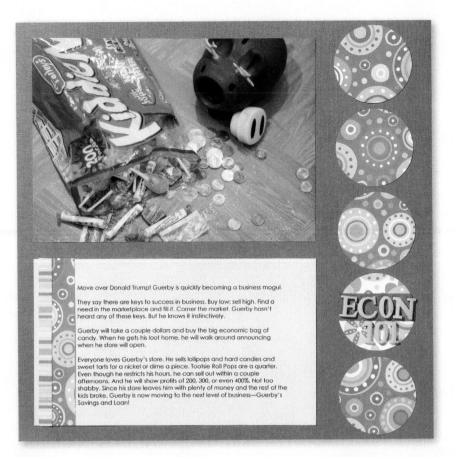

Simple

Elizabeth uses the sketch to give her title perfect placement on her page by using circles cut from a bold patterned paper. Elizabeth then ties in her journaling box with accents from the same patterned papers, creating a streamlined feel.

ECON 101
Elizabeth Ruuska, Rensselaer, Indiana

Supplies: Patterned paper (Paper Fever); textured cardstock (Bazzill); letters (Colorbök); circle punch (McGill)

Move over Donald Trump! Guerby is quickly becoming a business mogul.

They say there are keys to success in business. Buy low; sell high. Find a need in the marketplace and fill it. Corner the market. Guerby hasn't heard any of these keys. But he knows it instinctively.

Guerby will take a couple dollars and buy the big economic bag of candy. When he gets his loot home, he will walk around announcing when he store will open.

Everyone loves Guerby's store. He sells lollipops and hard candies and sweet tarts for a nickel or dime a piece. Tootsie Roll Pops are a quarter. Even though he restricts his hours, he can sell out within a couple afternoons. And he will show profits of 200, 300, or even 400%. Not too shabby. Since his store leaves him with plenty of money and the rest of the kids broke, Guerby is now moving to the next level of business—Guerby's Savings and Loan!

Enhanced

Kathy uses this sketch's spatial concept to apply many color-coordinated embellishments and papers, thereby enhancing the photo. A vibrant background lays the foundation for the remaining elements. Journaling and title are as the sketch calls for but enhanced to take on a style of their own.

MMM... CHOCOLATE
Kathy Fesmire, Athens, Tennessee

Supplies: Patterned papers (Anna Griffin, Current, Imagination Project, Making Memories, Memories in the Making); acrylic buckle, twill (Creek Bank Creations); mesh (Magic Mesh); metal floral accents (Hirschberg, Schutz & Co.); ribbon letters (PM Designs); foam alphabet stamps (Li'l Davis Designs, Making Memories); letter stamps (Making Memories, PrintWorks); date stamp (Memories in the Making); letter stickers (Pebbles); cardstocks; ribbons; staples; stamping ink; acrylic paint; brads

Reproducible Sketches

Here you'll find all of the single-photo sketches used in Chapter 1. Use these handy reproducible sketches to complete your own unique scrapbook pages, altering the sketch a tiny bit to fit your personal style or rotating the sketch to fit your layout needs. Simply photocopy the sketches, enlarging if desired to fit your sketch organizational system.

- PAGE **12** -

- PAGE **14** -

- PAGE **16** -

- PAGE **18** -

- PAGE **20** -

- PAGE **22** -

- PAGE **24** -

2- and 3-Photo
SKETCHES

chapter two

It's a well-known fact that the proper placement of photos, title and journaling on your page are among the most important factors in putting together a well-designed layout. For some of us, it can also be the one thing we struggle with the most. Placement of elements can be a very personalized thing reflecting a consistent, individual style. But for those of us who rearrange the elements on our page time and time again, it can turn into a level of frustration that takes some pleasure away from the hobby we love most.

Using sketches is one of the best things that's happened to scrapbookers because sketches give those who have gotten locked into a consistent design pattern the freedom to break away and change. Within this chapter you will find ideas on element placement that will leave you with the time and desire to get creative with titles, borders, journaling boxes and embellishments.

Remember that a sketch is only the starting point for your layout and while following the placement of elements provides the base for your page, the personalization of it is up to you. So pick a sketch and get started spending less time rearranging and more time creating awesome pages.

Danielle

Danielle has been Haley's best friend since kindergarten. In fact, we often joke about her being our weekend daughter because she spends most weekende at our house. She has a sweet spirit and kind soul and is a blessing to our entire family. We enjoy having her in our home and she and Haley seem to find endless things to do when they are together. When she first started coming over, they filled their time with coloring books, cartoons and hopscotch. Now that they are growing up, their time together is filled with lots of giggling, talk of boys, doing nails and trying their hand at putting on makeup. I can easily see them together years from now on prom night getting ready through the nervous laughter. I hope that they will continue to share the sweet bond of having that one special girlfriend to share everything with... there's nothing like it!

PHOTO

TITLE

JOURNALING

PHOTO

funny Face

Personality. Rebekah, you are certainly full of personality. When I get out the camera, you don't shy away from it like your brothers. I can almost hear you saying, "I'm ready for my close up now, Mr. DeVille." Your mood often determines the type of poses & facial expressions I'll get from you. Here you are being silly, but I also get photos of you when you are imagining you're a princess, poses of you as a dinosaur and even modeling shots when you want to show off your outfit or a particular leg lift. Where the camera is concerned, you surely are a ham. Despite your silliness, your sweet personality always shines through, even if you are blowing raspberries at me.

Blessed are the HAPPY makers.
~ Henry Ward Beecher

Graphic

Sheila personalizes the sketch by rounding the outside corners of the enlarged photos, the title and the journaling block. The journaling is slightly changed from the sketch by altering it to include a large quote block, adding visual interest.

FUNNY FACE
Sheila Doherty, Coeur d'Alene, Idaho

Supplies: Patterned paper, acrylic bauble (KI Memories); textured cardstock (Prism Papers); polka-dot tape (Heidi Swapp); wooden letter (Li'l Davis Designs); circle punch (McGill); corner rounder (Carl)

TITLE

JOURNALING

PHOTO

PHOTO

Simple

Angelia uses the sketch's ample journaling space to get creative. A circle is cut from patterned paper to place under her strip-style journaling, adding movement. To create separation, a coordinating strip of patterned paper is mounted down the center of the page at the photo's edges, a slight alteration from the sketch.

MY SISTER
Angelia Wigginton, Belmont, Mississippi

Supplies: Patterned papers (Chatterbox); leather flowers (Making Memories); letter stickers (Doodlebug Design); epoxy letters (K & Company); epoxy word, metal frame (Li'l Davis Designs); buttons; brads

Enhanced

Denise changes the sketch significantly by creating a dramatic focal photo with an oversized mat and ribbon embellishment. She overlaps her title onto her focal photo, re-emphasizing the photo's subject matter and drawing even more attention to it. The journaling is printed vertically as opposed to horizontally for an interesting visual effect.

ROYALTY
Denise Tucker, Versailles, Indiana

Supplies: Patterned paper (Basic Grey); embossed paper (Provo Craft); chipboard letters (Rusty Pickle); metal letters, colored staples (Making Memories); filigree embellishments (JewelCraft); rub-on letters (C-Thru Ruler); floral paper clip, buckle (Nunn Design); ribbons (Jo-Ann Stores, Making Memories, Offray, Wal-Mart); embossing powder; transparency; metallic jeweled trim; acrylic paint; brads; stamping ink

Graphic

Leah's design for the sketch included mounting cut sections from realistic printed papers with her enlarged focal photo. The placement of the photos is altered by mounting them onto the layout side by side, or overlapping, as opposed to giving each their own space—providing a seamless, graphic style.

18% GREY
Leah Blanco Williams, Rochester, New York

Supplies: Patterned papers (Hot Off The Press, Provo Craft, Wübie Prints); textured cardstock (Bazzill); asterisk punch (All Night Media); cardstock

They say that 18% grey is the shade of grey that photographers love best. Well, I had a tough decision to make when I had these pictures of flowers from my backyard developed. Color or black and white? That was the question. On one hand, grey would let a certain texture and rawness come out that color could not. On the other hand, I was afraid to lose that soft touch of pink and all those bright yellow centers. I wanted to capture it all—a special tribute to the flowers from my first house in Kansas City. I wanted to forever remember the excitement of seeing them bloom and the happiness of picking them at the just the right moment so they could grace our kitchen table. What was I thinking? Of course these things would not be lost. Their vibrant colors, the way they smelled, and the way they made me feel will be fresh in my memory because I'll hold them not in a photograph but close to my heart.

18% GRE*Y

Simple

Holly makes literal use of this sketch by housing all of her elements in boxes, allowing them to stand out on her busy background. To make the focal photo shine, colorful ribbons are placed on the right side along with rub-on words. Using more coordinating ribbons, she is able to tie her journaling and title boxes in with the main photo.

BACKYARD PLAY
Holly VanDyne, Mansfield, Ohio

Supplies: Patterned paper (Chatterbox); textured cardstock (Bazzill); letter stamps (PSX Design); rub-on letters (Autumn Leaves, Junkitz); ribbons (American Crafts); stamping ink

In Summer, 2004 our back yard became Audrey's playground. It was impossible for Audrey to go from the driveway straight to the house. The play gym was too tempting, and she would have to play for a while before she would ever come inside. The minute she caught a glimpse of that gym with its doors, windows, and super fun slide she wouldn't quit crying until she was playing on it.

Enhanced

Angie wanted to add a stylish twist to this sketch's concept and achieves it with a multilayered background. The placement of the photos, title and journaling stays true to the sketch but is enhanced with coordinating embellishments tying the whole page together.

FAMILY FUN
Angie Head, Friendswood, Texas
Photos: Family Memories, Friendswood, Texas

Supplies: Patterned papers, ID tags, green rivets (Chatterbox); ribbons (Bobbin Ribbon, Making Memories)

Graphic

Joanna benefited from the maximum journaling space provided by the sketch, altering it slightly to balance her page. For a graphic feel, photos were mounted side by side and then stabilized with computer-generated title and journaling. A ribbon is added across the center of the page, bringing together the layout.

CRACKED
Joanna Bolick, Fletcher, North Carolina

Supplies: Patterned paper (KI Memories); textured cardstocks (Bazzill); ribbon (Making Memories); image-editing software (Adobe Photoshop, Alien Skin Xenofex 2)

to keep in mind when dying eggs with a 2-year-old

- newspaper, preferably taped to the table and underneath the chairs, is a necessity
- a colorful liquid in a cup looks a lot like Koolaid, even if it smells like vinegar
- boiled eggs can only endure so much, especially when dropped into a cup from 2 feet above the table, or, for that matter, when simply thrown onto the floor in disgust
- there's no such thing as waiting patiently for eggs to turn colors
- eggs need to be inspected, sniffed, and handled frequently while still wet
- your helper will shake his head with a dejected look on his face and respond with "eggs...bwoke" when asked by Daddy about the egg-dying session

cracked
8.22.05

Simple

To maximize the space on her layout, Shelby uses a larger photo than indicated on the sketch as her focal point. The journaling on the layout is changed into strips as opposed to a block, keeping this sketch simple, yet altered to fit her style. A charming tag is added to tie in photos, journaling and title.

WHAT I SEE
Shelby Valadez, Saugus, California

Supplies: Textured cardstock, patterned paper (Chatterbox); patterned cardstock (Pebbles); metal-rimmed tag (Making Memories); phrase sticker (Wordsworth); ribbon; stamping ink; cardstock

(Layout text:)
{what I see}:
it's cold outside
a big brother helping out his little brother
two boys who stand out against the dreary day in their bright, warm clothing.
I especially love the yellow boots, hat and gloves.
two boys who are a part of my family, a part of my life, always.
two boys who I love dearly and miss daily.

Enhanced

Bay maximized the journaling space allowed on this sketch with three different boxes that tell one story. To add visual interest, the photos are double matted and accents added. She adheres an embellished ribbon across the page and under the title, giving a sense of separation. It is balanced out with a button border on the bottom to complete the page.

YOU'RE A PRETTY BIRD
Bay Loftis, Philadelphia, Tennessee

Supplies: Patterned papers (American Crafts); textured cardstock (Club Scrap); watermark ink (Tsukineko); pigment powder (Ranger); ribbon charm (Junkitz); gold leafing pen (Krylon); die-cut letters (Accu-Cut); ribbon (Bobbin Ribbon); threads (Scrapworks, Yasutomo & Co.); skeleton leaves (Graphic Products Corp.); beads (Halcraft); stamping ink; buttons; tiles; transparency

(Layout text:)

You're a pretty BIRD

The Bird Who Owns Woodrow

Vital Statistics
Species: Budgerigar
Variation: Near-white
Name: Orlando
Gender: Female (surprise!)
Age: About 17 months
Size: One ounce, & 7 inches long
Joined the flock: January, 2004
Regular diet: Zupreem fruit pellets & a little seed mix
Favorite treats: Millet, rice, apples
Favorite toy: ActiviToys Ring Toss, white swing ring, Jingle Bell Roll
Named after: Favorite vacation spot
Owner: Woodrow, age 12

"They are enchanting."
When I asked Wesley what he would say about Woodrow and Orlando, that's what he said. "They just love each other."

And really – they are *enchanted*. I've never seen a boy and a bird so happy together. They're a match made in heaven – for now. Soon enough, Woodrow will outgrow his bond with the pale yellow budgie, and I'll have to get used to, I don't know, cars or girlfriends or something. But for now, Orlando is enough.

We got the budgie at Strictly Feathers just for Woodrow. For several months, Orlando lived in his room, but we've moved her cage to the bird room so she can hang out with the rest of the flock. Still, whenever she hears Woodrow or sees him, she calls for his attention.

And he gives it to her willingly. Every morning when he wakes up, he takes care of Orlando before he gets his own breakfast. He cleans out her food and water dishes, talking to her the whole time. He cleans the bottom of the

cage without complaint. He changes her toys regularly. He's just a very attentive bird owner.

Orlando returns the favor by just adoring Woodrow. If I reach for her, she fusses vehemently at me. I'm not her person.

Woodrow is hers. She talks to him earnestly, although we can barely understand "You're a pretty bird," and she lavishes him with kisses (even when he has chapped lips) and long preening sessions to tidy up his hair.

For the rest of us, Orlando is an absolute delight. She's incredibly agile and playful, swinging madly on her swing until she can catch the roof of her cage and dangle there. She loves to listen to the canary and whistling CD's, although she doesn't whistle a lot herself. She's quite fond of my cockatiel Guido and fusses if I take him out of her sight.

But I know she would trade all of us for just Woodrow. They are enchanted, after all – with each other only. And that's better than cars or girlfriends any day of the week.

Moose & Rabbit

Montana *wildlife*

On our Montana summer vacation in 2004, we decided to do a little hiking in the mountains. Just outside of Red Lodge there are miles and miles of hiking trails.

We were hoping to see some wildlife on the trail. We soon discovered that the tourists outnumbered the wildlife and that Jordan isn't much of a hiker.

Our hike in the Absaroka-Beartooth Wilderness wasn't a complete bust. Although we didn't see any real wild animals, Jordan had fun making funny animal ears on Dad.

Graphic

Jodi augments the graphic look of the sketch with a strip of patterned paper mounted on the center of the page separating it into quadrants. A subtitle is added to the strip for interest. Mesh is used to accentuate the page and the photos.

MOOSE & RABBIT
Jodi Heinen, Sartell, Minnesota

Supplies: Patterned paper (Chatterbox); textured cardstocks (Bazzill); mesh (Magic Mesh)

Simple

Sheryl applies the sketch concept to her layout with a few simple changes to give her the necessary space for the photos she wanted to use. The journaling was put on a tag and overlapped with a wider photo than was indicated on the sketch, bringing your eye to it. The title was extended down the side of the page for more visual interest.

YELLOWSTONE LAKE

Sheryl Highsmith, Fort Collins, Colorado
Photos: Michael Highsmith,
Fort Collins, Colorado

Supplies: Patterned paper (Daisy D's); textured cardstock (Bazzill); leather frames (Making Memories); metal charms (Pebbles); rub-on letters (Doodlebug Design, Making Memories); brads; vellum; floss; ribbon

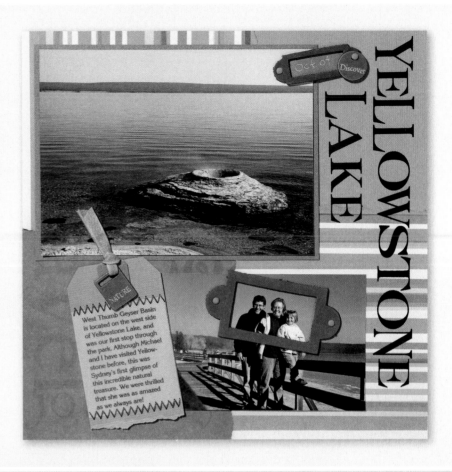

Enhanced

With the placement of the photos following the sketch, Colleen is able to augment the layout with her personal style of lots of dimensional embellishments. The title on the sketch is altered, turning the area into a visually perceived space as opposed to a visually blocked space, by maximizing the space the title occupies. The journaling block jumps off the page by using layers of embellishments under a transparency overlay.

DEEP SOUL

Colleen Macdonald, Winthrop,
West Australia, Australia

Supplies: Patterned paper (Basic Grey); chipboard letters, rub-on letters (Li'l Davis Designs); letter stickers (Provo Craft); Circa plaque (Card Connection); gold leaf embellishments (Beads & Plenty More); rattan place mat remnant; ribbon; poppy leaves; gold beads; beaded chain; stamping ink

Graphic

Ronnie creates a digital layout based on this sketch using a rickrack element to lead your eye around the page. The title is altered slightly by overlapping it onto the main photo. To further emphasize the focal photo, she attaches her journaling with a virtual brad completing her layout.

A REAL SWIMMER
Ronnie McCray, St. James, Missouri

Supplies: Image-editing software (Adobe Photoshop Elements 2.0); rickrack (www.tandika.com)

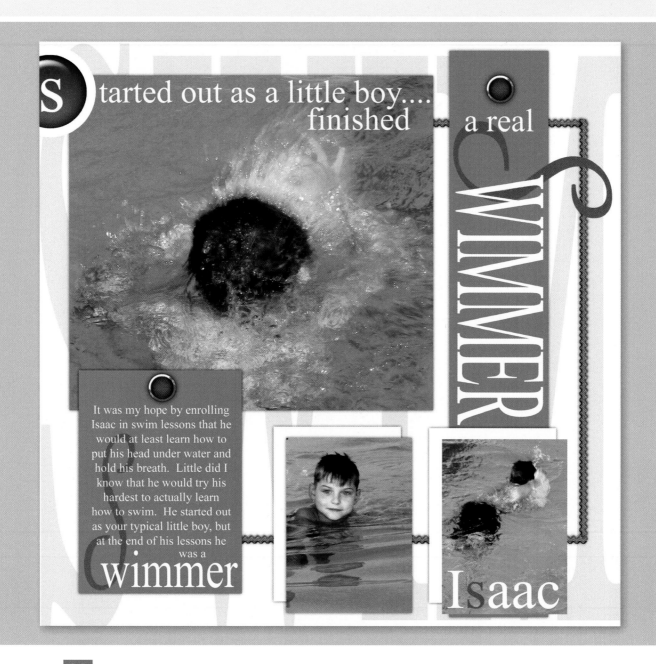

Simple

Emily stays with the sketch's placement but adjusts her use of space slightly to create a more balanced look for her photos. To fill space around her main photo and showcase it, a double mat is used along with a checkered ribbon for accent. She adds a photo to the title bar as opposed to making them separate elements as on the sketch. To complete her layout, embellishments are added to her extended journaling box that mirror the headlights on the car.

MEXICO 17-37-TRJ
Emily Curry Hitchingham,
Memory Makers Books

Supplies: Patterned paper (Basic Grey); number and state stickers (Sticker Studio); conchos (Jest Charming); epoxy stickers (K & Company); cardstock; ribbon

---

Enhanced

Diana completes her layout according to the sketch, drawing your attention to her main photo with a pretty embossed acrylic frame. Patterned papers were layered for a unique background, breaking up the graphic feel of the sketch. For variety, Diana keeps the placement of the title the same as the sketch but makes it smaller and places it horizontally on a tag.

DANCING FLOWER
Diana Hudson, Bakersfield, California

Supplies: Patterned papers (Anna Griffin, Autumn Leaves, Carolee's Creations); patterned vellums (Club Scrap, Paper Adventures); embossed acrylic frame (Carolee's Creations); flower sequins (Doodlebug Design); rub-on letters, metal-rimmed tags (Making Memories); flower punch (source unknown); mini brads (Lasting Impressions); sequins; acrylic paint

Graphic

Holly adds button-embellished boxes on the sides of her photos to give a better sense of balance to the sketch. Two different sizes are used on the expanded title to keep it appealing. Holly "pops" the journaling box to give the layout a little more character.

3 BOYS
Holly Corbett, Central, South Carolina

Supplies: Textured cardstocks (Bazzill); stem stamp (Hero Arts); mini buttons (Lasting Impressions); die-cut letters (QuicKutz); stamping ink

Simple

Ginger uses the sketch's concept to make the most of her focal photo, journaling and accents. The focal photo is mounted on an oversized mat and accented with acrylic paint. Adding to the sketch, Ginger fills some of the white space on her page using coordinating elements.

ART EXPRESS(ION)
Ginger McSwain, Cary, North Carolina

Supplies: Textured cardstocks (Bazzill); wooden train embellishment (EK Success); art/paint set embellishment (Keepsake Miniatures); bottle caps (ScrapGoods); bottle cap words (Club Scrap); label maker (Dymo); acrylic paint; paint chip

Enhanced

Diana enhances her page without compromising the sketch's concept by making small but effective changes. Two vertical photos are used in place of horizontal ones, bringing the attention to the focal photo in the center. The space permitted for the title allows Diana to get creative with its composition.

DEAREST
Diana Graham, Barrington, Illinois

Supplies: Patterned papers, tags (Basic Grey); pearl heart, wooden frame, chipboard letter (Li'l Davis Designs); coaster (SEI); metal letter, rub-on letters (Making Memories); word charm (source unknown); ribbons; transparency

The weather was awful, a summer shower soaked us all prior to arriving for the wedding rehearsal at the church. Afterward, the rain continued, but Rebecca and Robbie refused to let it ruin their celebration. The rehearsal dinner was decked out in purple accents, and the food was a gourmet buffet. I made the hats for the bride and groom, but I never actually expected them to wear them. I was shocked to find them sporting my gag gift throughout the night. I hope you two will always be as happy and as playful. So many people love you both.

REBECCA AND ROBBIE

REHEARSAL DINNER

6-5-04

Graphic

Danielle alters the straight lines of the sketch by rotating one of her supporting photos for visual interest on her digital layout. The placement of the elements stays true to the sketch, rendering a graphic feel, and is enhanced with a monochromatic background that complements the colors of the photos.

REHEARSAL DINNER
Danielle Layton, Clarksville, Tennessee

Supplies: Image-editing software (Microsoft Picture It!)

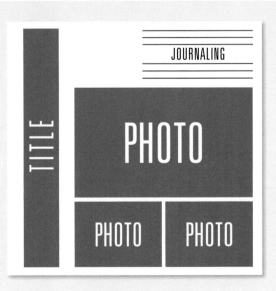

JOURNALING

TITLE

PHOTO

PHOTO   PHOTO

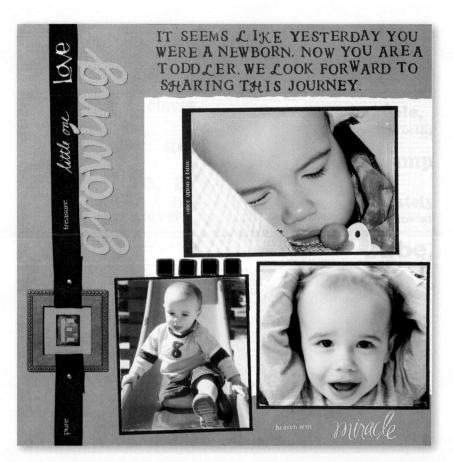

IT SEEMS LIKE YESTERDAY YOU WERE A NEWBORN. NOW YOU ARE A TODDLER. WE LOOK FORWARD TO SHARING THIS JOURNEY.

growing

love

little one

treasure

pure

once upon a time

heaven sent

miracle

Simple

Stacey uses slightly smaller photos than indicated on the sketch, giving her more freedom to get creative on the rest of the page. The title is applied on the left side of the layout and accented with a ribbon, a metal frame and rub-on words. To add her personal style to the sketch, she sands the photos' edges and then mounts them slightly off-center over patterned paper.

GROWING
Stacey Wakelin, Surrey, British Columbia, Canada

Supplies: Patterned paper (7 Gypsies); metal stencil letter, letter brads (Colorbök); letter stamps (PSX Design); metal frame, rub-on letters and sayings (Making Memories); die-cut letters (QuicKutz); ribbon (May Arts); cardstock; brads

Enhanced

Tonya uses the sketch's photo, title and journaling placement as a backbone for creating a vibrant computer-generated layout. Layers of textures for her background provide a unique setting for the remaining page elements. By placing embellishments and photos as the sketch indicates, but slightly off-center, Tonya creates a page that is unique to her style.

FACE 2 FACE
Tonya Doughty, Wenatchee, Washington

Supplies: Image-editing software (Adobe Photoshop CS); background paper, title, wooden word strips (Gauchogirl Creative)

You are full of curiousity, so much so that I am as equally exasperated as I am enthralled. One hundred questions a week (it seems) easily turns into that many in a single day when we go somewhere to engage your fertile young mind. Don't change a thing, baby. Soak it up. Be a sponge.

2004-Indy at the Seattle Aquarium

FACE 2 FACE

DISCOVER
IMAGINE
DREAM

Graphic

Michelle wanted to give her digital layout a grungy feel by altering the sketch with virtual elements. The placement of the photos, title and journaling stays true to the sketch and is enhanced with paint and texture effects, adding dimension to the layout.

MY PASSIONS
Michelle Shefveland, Sauk Rapids, Minnesota

Supplies: Image-editing software (Adobe Photoshop Elements 3.0); digital background (CottageArts.net)

Simple

Holle utilizes patterned paper that works perfectly with the sketch, allowing her to keep her layout quick and easy while still producing a darling page. To draw your eye to the focal photo, various ribbons are tied to the mat. She varied her title slightly from the sketch by using an oval section atop the title bar and extended it into her journaling.

IF WE BUILD IT, HE WILL COME
Holle Wiktorek, Reunion, Colorado

Supplies: Patterned paper (Sandylion); letter stamps (La Pluma, PSX Design); cardstock; stamping ink

Enhanced

Tricia uses a collage technique to complete a layout based on her version of the sketch. Placement of the elements stays the same but is kicked up a notch with embellishments. The smaller photos on the bottom of the sketch are placed together inside a transparency filmstrip on the layout for a unique twist. Accents are added in the blank space of the sketch to balance the page out and finish it.

SATURDAY PLAY
Tricia Rubens, Castle Rock, Colorado

Supplies: Patterned papers (Daisy D's, Design Originals, K & Company, Rusty Pickle); game piece letters and charms (Rusty Pickle, Westrim); postage stickers, woven label (Me & My Big Ideas); die-cut watch (DMD); filmstrip transparency (Creative Imaginations); metal photo corners, picture hanger (Daisy D's); hand-shaped clip, watch charms (Ink It); key charm (Boutique Trims); decorative brad (Making Memories); decorative paper clip (EK Success); metal clip (7 Gypsies); brads

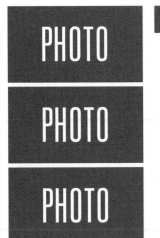

Graphic

Janice sticks with the graphic feel of the layout but adds bold color and embellishments to reflect her own style. The title is added to the journaling block for continuity, and black buttons are added to the bottom as accents, providing visual interest.

AMUSED

Janice Carson, Hamilton, Ontario, Canada

Supplies: Textured cardstock (Bazzill); buttons (Doodlebug Design)

AMUSED

One of my fondest childhood memories was our family trips to Fantasy Island Amusement park on Grand Island, New York.

We usually went on Thanksgiving weekend and stayed in our trailer at the campground next door. During the day we walked to the park to enjoy the rides. The park was never busy in October.

During July of 2002, we visited Fantasy Island for the first time with our own family. Jonathan was still young and stayed home with Nana.

It was really interesting to see that many of the same attractions still existed thirty years later. We rode the little train around the park (my favourite ride as a child). We sat in the potatoe sacks to speed down the huge slide. The Wild West show was fun and still as loud as I remembered.

Patrick particularly enjoyed the petting zoo. For the first time ever he wasn't afraid of the animals. In fact, he was quite captivated with the horses.

The last part of the day was spent in a "newer" Area of Fantasy Island...the water park. All of us piled onto our tubes to ride the Lazy River. Then it was off to the wave pool.

We can't wait until next year when Jonathan is old enough to enjoy the park.

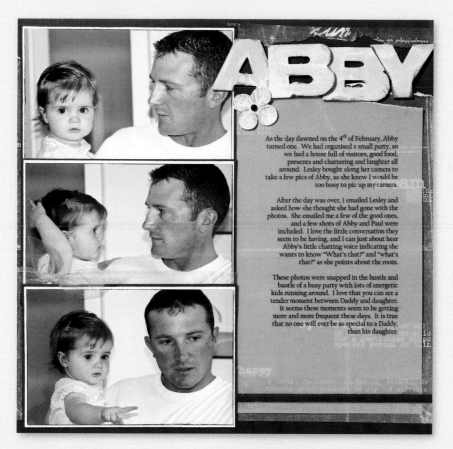

As the day dawned on the 4th of February, Abby turned one. We had organised a small party, so we had a house full of visitors, good food, presents and chattering and laughter all around. Lesley bought along her camera to take a few pics of Abby, as she knew I would be too busy to pic up my camera.

After the day was over, I emailed Lesley and asked how she thought she had gone with the photos. She emailed me a few of the good ones, and a few shots of Abby and Paul were included. I love the little conversation they seem to be having, and I can just about hear Abby's little chatting voice indicating she wants to know "What's that?" and "what's that?" as she points about the room.

These photos were snapped in the hustle and bustle of a busy party with lots of energetic kids running around. I love that you can see a tender moment between Daddy and daughter. It seems these moments seem to be getting more and more frequent these days. It is true that no one will ever be as special to a Daddy, than his daughter.

Simple

Nic follows this sketch's placement of photos, title and journaling but adds little accents, bringing special focus to each one. To showcase her focal photo in the center, a sheer ribbon is tied around it. She then accents the journaling box with the same ribbon to tie the elements together. To draw your eye toward the title, a pretty floral accent is added, completing her layout.

ABBY

Nic Howard, Pukekone, South Auckland, New Zealand
Photos: Lesley Cooper, Te Atatu Peninsular, Auckland, New Zealand

Supplies: Patterned paper (Pebbles); chipboard letters, paper flower (Making Memories); vellum; ribbon; cardstock; stamping ink; acrylic paint

Enhanced

Cherie uses the sketch's appealing arrangement of photos to showcase her attractive flower prints. To give her title more impact, she enlarges part of it then enhances the letters with colored pencils. Adorning her page with several ribbons and metal accents provides a beautiful end result to the sketch.

MOSS ROSES

Cherie Ward, Colorado Springs, Colorado

Supplies: Patterned paper, letter stickers (Basic Grey); textured cardstocks (Bazzill); tag (Pebbles); metal flower charms (All My Memories); colored pencils (Sanford); letter stamps (Stamp Craft); ribbon (Offray); stamping ink; staples

Reproducible Sketches

Here you'll find all of the two- and three-photo sketches used in Chapter 2. Use these handy reproducible sketches to complete your own unique scrapbook pages, altering the sketch a tiny bit to fit your personal style or rotating the sketch to fit your layout needs. Simply photocopy the sketches, enlarging if desired to fit your sketch organizational system.

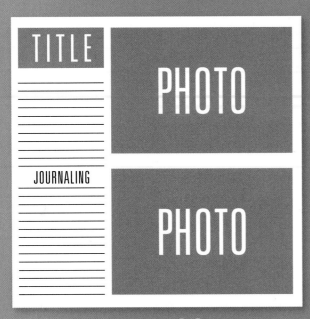

- PAGE **30** -

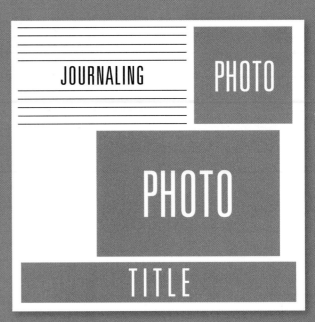

- PAGE **32** -

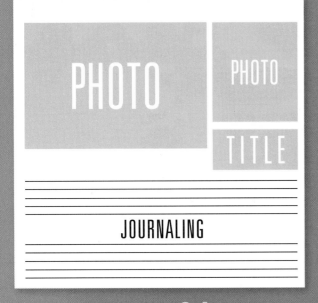

- PAGE **34** -

- PAGE **36** -

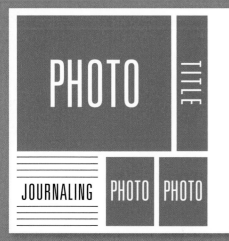

- PAGE **38** -

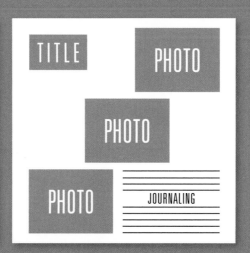

- PAGE **40** -

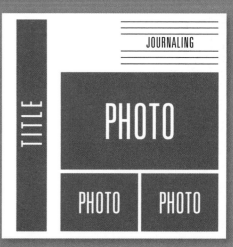

- PAGE **42** -

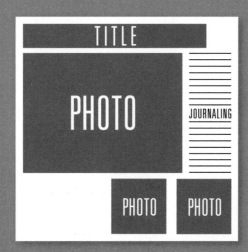

- PAGE **44** -

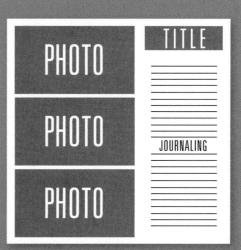

- PAGE **46** -

4- and 5-Photo
SKETCHES

chapter three

Supporting photos are at times as important to the layout as the focal photo because they often tell the remainder of the story. We use them to show other emotions, other perspectives and even other viewpoints of the same space in time. They become the visuals for our journaling and windows into the personalities behind the pictures.

Supporting photos can come in all shapes and sizes and can be mounted in many different ways. How they are placed on a page is as important as the context of the photos themselves. Placed incorrectly, they can distract from your main photo, causing you to lose not only balance on your page, but focus on your focal photo. Your challenge can come from trying to decide how and where to place them without muddying your layout and distracting from the other elements.

This chapter of sketches helps you make that decision by giving you the ability to highlight your main photo as well as tell a story with your supporting photos and still create a well-balanced and stylish layout. Use these sketches and ideas from the artists to help you tell the next important story behind your main photo.

When we all got together for Grandpa's birthday, it didn't take much to convince the kids to let me shoot some photos. They were in the backyard horsing around and piling on each other before I could get the camera out of the bag. They really put the "ham" in Hammond and it's plain to see the silly gene is getting passed down to this generation as well. None of them seem to be too camera shy!

PHOTO

PHOTO

PHOTO

TITLE

PHOTO

JOURNALING

Graphic

Using the sketch to place her elements, MaryAnn completes her digital layout, adding personal touches to show her own style. To draw your eye toward the focal photo, it is matted on a red background that includes her journaling below and a dotted accent down the left side. The smaller photos are tied in to the journaling with dotted lines separating each of them, giving her layout a graphic feel.

OUR FAVORITE BEACH
MaryAnn Wise, The Woodlands, Texas

Supplies: Image-editing software (Adobe Photoshop); background paper and elements (Rhonna Farrer kit from www.twopeasinabucket.com)

We loved spending the Fourth of July holiday at the beach. Celebrating our country's freedom in the sand and salt water at Gulfshores Baptist Assembly was a much-needed family getaway. Kaitlyn and Addison had so much fun and enjoyed a little taste of independence on their own!

Simple

To stay true to the sketch but add dimension and texture, Valerie uses theme-coordinating ribbons around her title and focal photo. The title is reduced to allow room for the wider flag ribbon, and the journaling box is accented with patriotic bottle caps and red ribbon. To complete the layout, red ribbon is added below the focal photo and a rub-on word atop the photo, truly bringing your eye to it.

LET FREEDOM RING
Valerie Barton, Flowood, Mississippi

Supplies: Bottle caps (Jest Charming); metal letter tags (DieCuts with a View); letter stickers (Creative Imaginations); rub-on word (Making Memories); ribbon (SEI); cardstock; colored brads

Enhanced

Courtney uses the sketch to showcase enlarged photos and alters the journaling to make it her own unique style. The center photo on the left row of photos is enlarged to spotlight it while the focal photo is matted to draw attention to it. She alters the title by placing it vertically down the page and then horizontally on center, drawing your eye along the page. The journaling is hidden under ribbons and cardstock located below the photo for a unique change to the sketch.

DREAM BIG
Courtney Walsh, Winnebago, Illinois

Supplies: Patterned papers (Chatterbox, Mustard Moon); rivets, letter stickers, printed tag (Chatterbox); ribbon (May Arts); cardstocks; stamping ink; staples

The future belongs to those who believe in the beauty of their dreams.
Eleanor Roosevelt

Graphic

To complement the strong vertical and horizontal lines in this sketch, Kimberly layers ribbon on the left side with her title and along the bottom with her journaling. For a glitzy look, a rhinestone buckle is added on the bottom ribbon. The title stays as the sketch indicates, but is pumped up with cut and layered circles and letter stickers.

SUPER MODEL
Kimberly Kesti, Phoenix, Arizona

Supplies: Patterned paper (SEI); rhinestone buckle (Li'l Davis Designs); letter stickers (American Crafts); ribbon (Strano Designs); cardstock

super model

Introducing....Meghan Esther...supermodel! Well, she is for me, at least. I have to give Meghan a lot of credit. She cheerfully poses for my endless photo shoots, helps me with backgrounds and lighting, and finally does lots of babysitting for her younger siblings while Mom scraps the night away! Model, or no, I think this girl is one beautiful daughter, helper and most of all, friend.

Simple

Kathy makes simple and easy changes to the sketch that make a big impact on the end result of her page. The title bar is enhanced with layered torn and inked patterned papers, rub-ons, ribbons and bottle cap embellishments, creating an intricate look. The smaller photos on the sketch are made slightly longer and are mounted side by side on the page, while the focal photo is reduced to make room for an embellishment.

PIECES OF OUR SWEET BABY GIRL
Kathy Fesmire, Athens, Tennessee
Photos: Joan Standridge, Athens, Tennessee

Supplies: Patterned papers (Design Originals, Memories Complete); paint strip, sanding block (PM Designs); bottle caps, bottle cap stickers (Design Originals); lace sticker (Sandylion); letter stickers (Chatterbox, Mrs. Grossman's); rub-on words (DieCuts with a View, Making Memories); date stamp (Memories in the Making); acrylic label holder (Creek Bank Creations); ribbons (Offray); silk flower; metallic paint; transparency; stamping ink

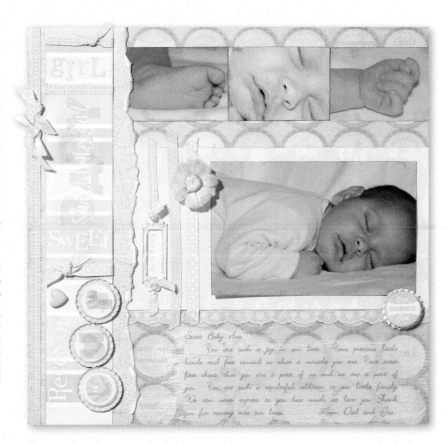

Enhanced

Jeniece enhances this sketch with changes to the title and smaller photos to fit her artistic style. The title is layered with painted and stitched patterned paper and a computer-printed transparency. As opposed to three smaller photos above the focal photo as it appears on the sketch, she stitches a large patterned paper border piece across the top of the layout and mounts the photos along with painted key accents.

SWEET PRINCESS SUITE
Jeniece Higgins, Lake Forest, Illinois

Supplies: Patterned papers, chipboard frame (Rusty Pickle); key accents (Li'l Davis Designs); foam alphabet stamps (Making Memories); ribbon (Offray, Rusty Pickle); acrylic paint; transparency

Graphic

Susan stays with the clean look of the sketch's photo, title and journaling placement, but adds her own touch by vaguely altering the look of the elements on the page. For her title, vellum letters are mounted on cardstock then rounded at the corners. To stay with that look, she rounds the outside corners of her focal photo, supporting photo and journaling box for a sleek design.

CLOWNIN'
Susan Cyrus, Broken Arrow, Oklahoma

Supplies: Textured cardstocks (Bazzill); metal-rimmed tag (Making Memories); die-cut flower (KI Memories); patterned vellum (American Crafts); cardstock; rickrack

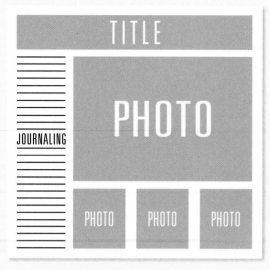

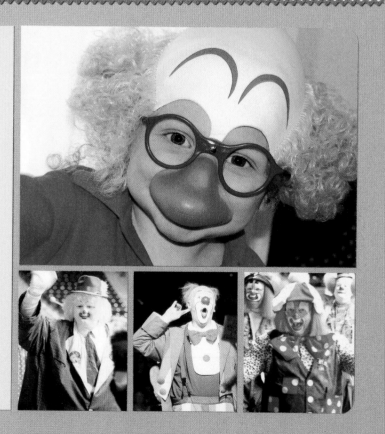

The **best** clown of the Akdar Shrine Circus was the one we brought from home!

February 2005

Simple

Denise uses the journaling space provided on the sketch to add a subtitle and embellishments for her Halloween layout. To unify the bottom three photos and slightly modify the sketch, she mats all of them onto a single mat. To draw your eye to the focal photo, a vellum accent is added on the top of the page and under the photo.

HOOSIER HALLOWEEN
Denise Tucker, Versailles, Indiana

Supplies: Patterned paper (Basic Grey, Rusty Pickle); metal frame and letters, wooden letters (Westrim); die-cut letters (Sizzix); embossing powder; cardstock; transparency; vellum; brads

Enhanced

Stacy varies this sketch by altering the focal photo, journaling and title to echo her own style. The title is broken up into two sections as opposed to a single section, providing an area for a subtitle. For visual interest, the journaling block is cut into a curve that is mirrored on the top right side of the layout with cut cardstock. She then uses a vertical focal photo, giving her room on her page for more embellishments.

GO FISH
*Stacy McFadden,
Park Orchards, Victoria, Australia*

Supplies: Textured cardstock (Bazzill); leather flowers, photo turns (Making Memories); wooden letter (Lincraft); rub-on letters (Rusty Pickle); letter tiles (Collections, Scrapworks); ribbon (May Arts); brads; stamping ink

My *SISTER*

Rebecca is *Beautiful* and **FUN**.

She is **THOUGHTFUL** and *Affectionate*.

She makes me laugh, she is so *Witty*.

She is a **Dog lover** through and through. She has a *Brave* ♡.

Graphic

Danielle follows the sketch precisely to make her digital layout show off all of the important elements. For the journaling, different fonts are used to add visual variety. To better define the space, she adds a border around the entire layout, tightening it all up.

MY SISTER
Danielle Layton, Clarksville, Tennessee

Supplies: Image-editing software (Microsoft Picture It!)

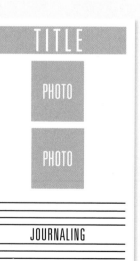

Simple

Becky adapts this sketch to fit her larger photos by altering the placement of the title, giving her the room she needs. Attention to the focal photo is made with an oversized mat and ribbon accent. Placement of the supporting photos on the sketch moves on the page and makes the title sit on the top right corner of the page as opposed to above the photos as on the sketch.

FLY HIGH

Becky Thompson, Fruitland, Idaho

Supplies: Patterned paper (SEI); rub-on letters (Making Memories; Me & My Big Ideas); ribbon (Offray); cardstock

A spring day in Idaho. There's nothing quite like it. Those first rays of sunshine after the cold chill of winter are such a welcome change of pace. January & February's fog and grey are replaced by the gentle warm breezes and bright warm sunlight of March. The grass just begins to change from brown to green, and the trees begin to bud out in preparation for the summer canvas of shade they will provide. With all that at your disposal, you can't help but want to get outside, climb into a tire swing, and let yourself fly.

The field of flowers was absolutely gorgeous and you had such a wonderful time walking through them and picking a beautiful handful of them! Your innocence shined so brightly to me on this day and I was so very thankful for the beautiful little girl God has blessed our life with. I love you with all my heart, Kiersten.

Enhanced

Heather personalizes this sketch with a pleasurable border on the bottom of the page and a unique multimedia title. The larger photos on the sketch are matted on the layout and separated with a ribbon and wooden flower accent. The supporting photos are cropped smaller than on the sketch, leaving room for a larger artistic title, a smaller journaling box and a fun layered ribbon and transparency border.

SPRING

Heather Preckel, Swannanoa, North Carolina

Supplies: Patterned paper (K & Company); textured cardstock (Bazzill); wooden flower, chipboard letter (Lil' Davis Designs); letter buttons (Junkitz); letter stencil (Autumn Leaves); ribbon (Making Memories, Michaels); brads; rickrack; transparency; button; stamping ink

Graphic

Sheila uses the photo placement on the sketch to further enhance her prints by framing the group on a large patterned paper mat. Instead of placing the title by itself as the sketch indicates, she integrates it into her journaling. For balance, acrylic embellishments are adhered on opposite corners of the page.

CHRISTMAS BABY
Sheila Doherty, Coeur d'Alene, Idaho

Supplies: Patterned paper (Karen Foster Design, KI Memories); textured cardstock (Prism Papers); acrylic embellishments (KI Memories); ribbon (Michaels)

PHOTO	PHOTO
PHOTO	PHOTO

TITLE

JOURNALING

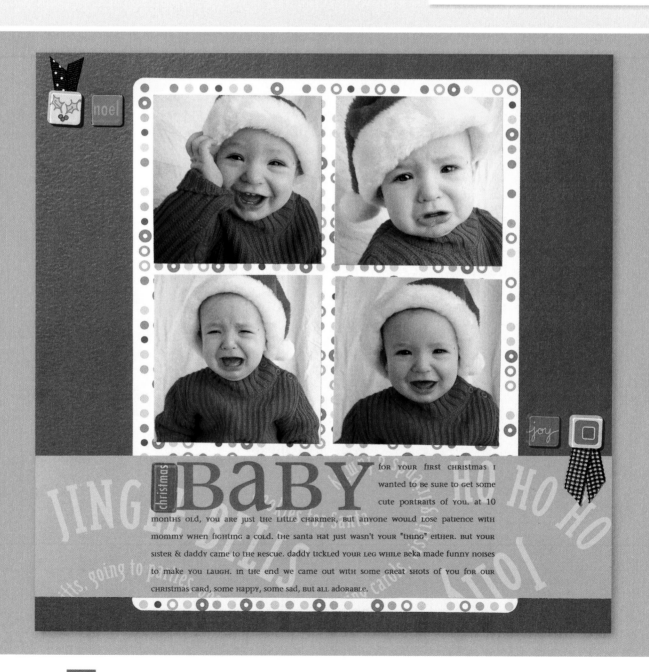

christmas **BABY** for your first christmas i wanted to be sure to get some cute portraits of you. at 10 months old, you are just the little charmer, but anyone would lose patience with mommy when fighting a cold. the santa hat just wasn't your "thing" either. but your sister & daddy came to the rescue. daddy tickled your leg while beka made funny noises to make you laugh. in the end we came out with some great shots of you for our christmas card, some happy, some sad, but all adorable.

Simple

Samuel slightly off-centers the photos to somewhat contrast the sketch. Circles are used for the title to reflect "water fun" and are placed at the bottom of the page where the sketch placed journaling. To further differ from the sketch, Samuel used a tag to journal on, which is mounted on the bottom left of the page.

SOAKED
Samuel Cole, Stillwater, Minnesota

Supplies: Patterned papers (Anna Griffin, Bella Press, Carolee's Creations, Creative Imaginations, KI Memories); epoxy circle, circle punch (EK Success); letter stamps (Hero Arts, Stampabilities); swirl stamp (Hero Arts); tag (DMD); ribbon (Michaels); cardstock; stamping inks

Enhanced

To break up the squared style of the sketch, Julie rounds the outside corners of her photos and uses cut circles from patterned paper on her background. Chipboard letters provide a unique title and are mounted above the journaling just as the sketch illustrates. Julie continues her index tabs beneath her photos and title with fitting synonyms.

EXPRESSIONS
Julie Johnson, Seabrook, Texas

Supplies: Patterned paper (Chatterbox); textured cardstock (Prism Papers); synonym tabs (Autumn Leaves); mini file clips (Karen Foster Design); word embellishment, letter stamps, chipboard letters (Making Memories); stamping ink; brads

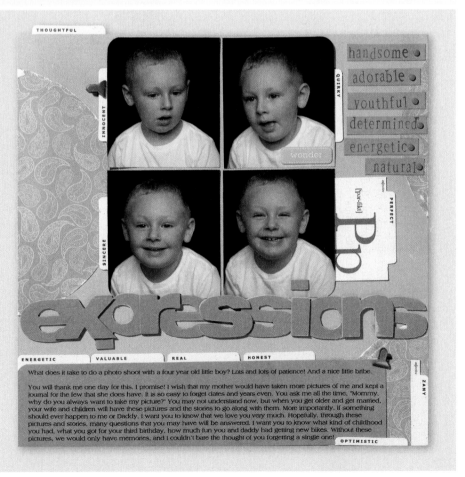

Graphic

Jessie uses the placement of the smaller supporting photos on the sketch to balance out her main photo and larger title. The journaling is applied directly on the blocks of the patterned paper with rub-on words, and handwritten words added by Jessie work perfectly for her boyish layout.

STAY THIS WAY
Jessie Baldwin, Las Vegas, Nevada

Supplies: Patterned paper (Basic Grey); letter stickers (Making Memories, Mustard Moon); rub-on words (Making Memories); cardstock; twill

Simple

Nicole maintains most of the sketch's design, taking advantage of the space to get creative with her title. The smaller photo is framed with a metal-rimmed tag to draw attention to it and then added to part of the title box, keeping the layout simple and appealing.

DISCOVERING SEA TURTLE
Nicole Cholet,
Beaconsfield, Quebec, Canada

Supplies: Textured cardstocks, chipboard pieces (Bazzill); square conchos (Scrapworks); metal-rimmed tag, rub-on letters (Making Memories); letter stamps (Hero Arts, Ma Vinci's Reliquary, PSX Design); photo corners (Canson); stamping ink

While on our vacation in Guadeloupe, we decided to go on an excursion to snorkel on one of the coral reefs around the island. We were taken on a gorgeous boat to an island that had been turned into a nature preserve. We were able to spend the day exploring the reef and a bit of the island itself. We saw some amazing fish, a shark, and thousands of hermit crabs but none of those could outdo the turtle that came up to the boat during lunch. The boys were up and finished eating in record time so they could hang out at the back of the boat and watch the turtle play around. I have to admit, it was pretty cool! I had never seen a sea turtle that large in it's natural habitat before - and never one so comfortable around people and boats. It stayed around the boat for quite some time, and the captain of the boat started feeding it some of the left over fish from lunch. The boys were so excited and they desperately wanted to feed the turtle too but after seeing how it snapped it's jaws onto the tongs the captain was using, we thought better of it. Disappointed? Yes, but they got over it quickly. It's hard to stay upset when something that cool is right there in front of you!

Enhanced

Angelia followed this sketch's placement exactly but stylizes it by plumping up the journaling box with embellishments to fill space she didn't need. Label stickers with phrases are added with button accents to complete the title. Bold colors and patterns bring out the colors in the photo for a perfect match and a lively layout.

BLISSFUL TREAT
Angelia Wigginton, Belmont, Mississippi

Supplies: Patterned papers, rub-on letters, label stickers (K & Company); stencil letter date stamp, buttons, mini brads (Making Memories); stamping ink

What can you say about a man who puts ketchup on EVERY-THING? In Scotty's case, you say "It's gotta be Heinz". Scotty puts ketchup on the oddest things. One of his favorite delicacies is ketchup, bacon, and peanut butter sandwiches. YUCK. I've never met anyone with such a palate for ketchup. Never. So don't be offended if he comes to your house for dinner and puts ketchup on his filet mignon.

Graphic

Torrey stays with the graphic style of the sketch but creates a unique look by merging a black-and-white photo layer with a circle-shaped color photo layer using image-editing software. The circle theme is extended with rounded photo corners and cardstock circles tucked beneath photos and as additional page design elements. She makes room for her bottle border by shifting the elements of the sketch to the upper left of the page.

KETCHUP
Torrey Scott, Thornton, Colorado

Supplies: Patterned papers (All My Memories, Doodlebug Design); image-editing software (Adobe Photoshop Elements); cardstock

Simple

Amy adapts the sketch just a tiny bit by varying the sizes of her photos enough to accommodate a larger journaling block and to showcase date and photo tags. The smaller photo is showcased on a metal-rimmed tag for added charm.

BLOOM
Amy Glander, Memory Makers Books
Photos: Edris Montalvo, Universal City, Texas

Supplies: Patterned paper (K & Company); flowers, leaves (Pressed Petals); metal-rimmed tag (Making Memories); die-cut letters (QuicKutz); ribbon (Michaels); cardstock; vellum; eyelets; pen

Enhanced

To get away from the graphic feel of the sketch, Trudy stitched on horizontal strips of vibrant fabrics for her background. To balance the page and draw your eye to the focal photo, vertical ribbon is added. She makes a flower-decorated title border to complete a layout that has her own personal style all over it.

GARDEN GIRL
Trudy Sigurdson,
Victoria, British Columbia, Canada

Supplies: Textured cardstock (Bazzill); letter stamps (Scraptivity Scrapbooking); rub-on letters (Chatterbox, Scrapworks); ribbon (Rusty Pickle); flowers (Hirschberg, Schutz, & Co.); cardstock; colored fabric strips; acrylic paint; gold pen

Graphic

Barb makes only slight variations to the graphic design of the sketch to achieve a lot of eye appeal on her layout. Smaller photos are grouped as in the sketch then double matted along with the focal photo. Charms strung on gingham ribbon are mounted nicely between them, adding an eye-catching touch. She adorns her title block with a silk flower to complete the layout.

THE SECOND GENERATION
Barb Hogan, Cincinnati, Ohio

Supplies: Patterned paper, rub-on letters (Imagination Project); textured cardstock (Bazzill); metal charms (Making Memories); ribbon (Offray); ribbon flower (Card Connection)

Simple

Dayna follows this sketch's placement concept but alters her photos to give her layout a less blocked appearance. The focal photo is tilted slightly for interest and the supporting photos are cut into circles as opposed to squares as indicated on the sketch. All are sanded and matted on one large section of torn paper and netting, bringing them all together on the page. She adds netting accents to her journaling to complete the layout.

NEWPORT
Dayna Gilbert, McMinnville, Oregon

Supplies: Patterned paper (Karen Foster Design); textured cardstock (Bazzill); metal letter (Making Memories); label holder, letter brads (Jo-Ann Stores); die-cut letter (Sizzix); metal sheet (AMACO); netting; stamping ink

Enhanced

Andrea uses gold trim not only to divide the sections of the sketch but to enhance them on her layout. Elements in the title block are brought into the journaling block for visual balance. Both are enhanced with beading and charms to create a striking layout.

ONCE UPON A TIME
Andrea Lyn Vetten-Marley, Aurora, Colorado
Photos: Eileen Bosko, Aurora, Colorado

Supplies: Clay (Polyform Products); pigment powders (Jacquard Products); watermark ink (Tsukineko); extra thick embossing powder (Ranger); letter stamps (Stampabilities); dragonfly charms (Hirschberg, Schutz, & Co.); beads (Blue Moon Beads); mulberry paper (DMD); fabric; gold trim; tulle; stamping ink

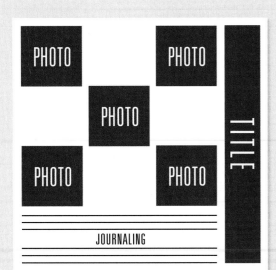

Graphic

Leah uses the space around the photos on the sketch to get creative and reflect her style. The photos and elements are mounted to the edge of the page as opposed to the placement on the sketch, allowing room for her title and ribbon accent. To fill the spaces around the photos, she punches theme-coordinating shapes and mounts them on punched squares. For a twist on her journaling, she uses strip-style journaling in place of a block.

SUSHI NIGHT
Leah Blanco Williams, Rochester, New York

Supplies: Patterned paper (source unknown); textured patterned paper (Paper Company); Asian punch wheel (Hyglo); Japanese rubber stamp (Leave Memories); geisha charm (Sarah Heidt Photo Craft); ribbon (Europa Imports); square punch (EK Success); embossing powder; cardstock; stamping ink

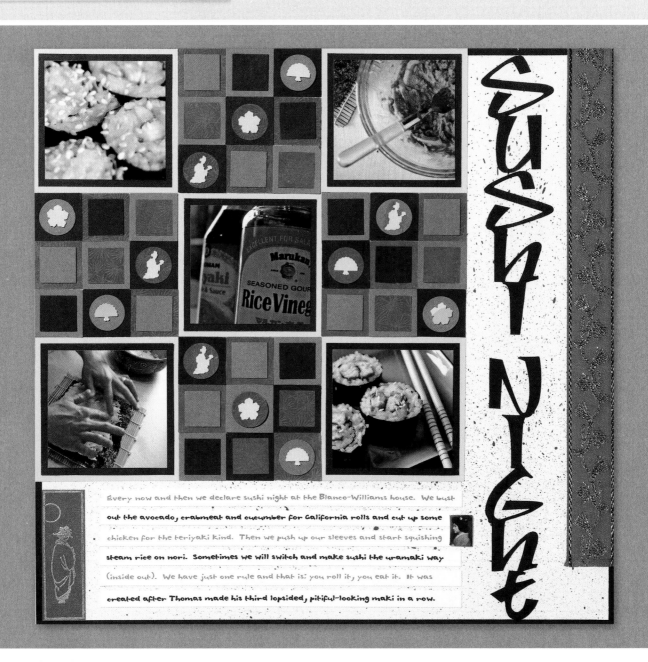

Simple

Jane uses the sketch's placement of photos to showcase many different pictures of one subject. A focal point is created from the center photo by double matting it against the same patterned cardstock she used to mat her entire layout. She uses a variety of colors for her title, tying it into the page. The placement of the title and journaling stays true to the sketch.

MAXWELL'S HATS
Jane Swanson, Janesville, Wisconsin

Supplies: Textured cardstocks (Bazzill, Club Scrap); metal picture hangers (Bull Dog); letter template (EK Success); colored brads (Making Memories); cardstock

Enhanced

Shannon adds to the sketch's concept by filling in the spaces around the photos with stitched, textured paper and leaf accents. The focal photo commands attention by using surrounding photos that do not distract from it. She stretches her journaling across the bottom of the page, slightly shortening her title, and enhances it with leaf accents.

ABUNDANCE
Shannon Taylor, Bristol, Tennessee

Supplies: Patterned paper (Scenic Route Paper Co.); textured papers (Bazzill, Eco-Africa); letter template (C-Thru Ruler); dimensional adhesive (JudiKins); pressed leaves (Pressed Petals); brads

Autumn brings an abundance of treasures to my world before winter takes it all away. Plenty of bright orange pumpkins; warm fuzzy sweaters; crunchy, colorful leaves; and crisp cool days bring a bit of joy to each of my days. I just can't believe I never experienced a true Fall until my 20th year of life.

Reproducible Sketches

Here you'll find all of the four- and five-photo sketches used in Chapter 3. Use these handy reproducible sketches to complete your own unique scrapbook pages, altering the sketch a tiny bit to fit your personal style or rotating the sketch to fit your layout needs. Simply photo-copy the sketches, enlarging if desired to fit your sketch organizational system.

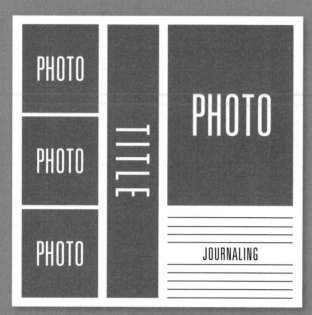

- PAGE **52** -

- PAGE **54** -

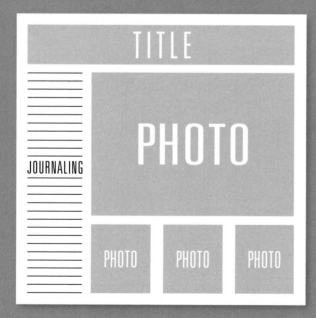

- PAGE **56** -

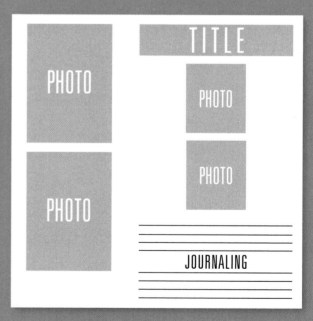

- PAGE **58** -

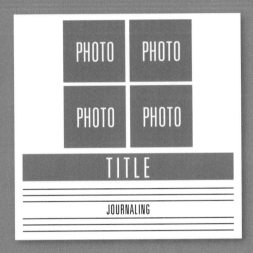

- PAGE **60** -

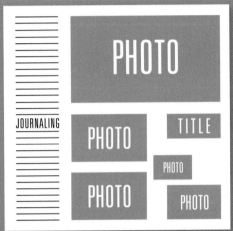

- PAGE **62** -

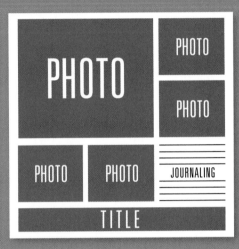

- PAGE **64** -

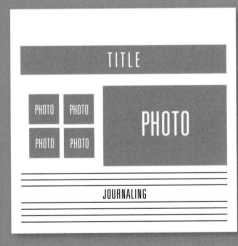

- PAGE **66** -

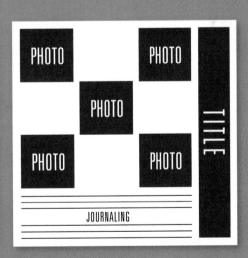

- PAGE **68** -

6- or More Photo
SKETCHES

chapter four

As scrapbookers, we all have been guilty of taking too many pictures of the same thing at one time or another. But how do we determine how many photos is too many photos, which get filed away and which get put in the scrapbook? It is a hard decision to make, but there is a solution. You can scrap them all!

Finding space for many photos on a single layout without cluttering your page and still finding room for a title, journaling and embellishments can prove to be a challenge for even the most seasoned scrapbookers. Quite often when using a lot of photos, we tend not to think about making them smaller to fit onto a smaller space. We often compromise journaling or a creative title to fit more photos instead of making one page a two-page spread.

The following chapter will show you how to avoid this difficulty and accomplish a sleek and neat, single-page layout even when you have more photos than room. You will see— based on the many sketches ahead and the artists' interpretations of them—that many photos can be placed on a single page to maximize your space and still allow room for creative titles, expressive journaling and great page accents. Now grab that pile of photos, find a sketch and get busy!

hicks

When Tom and Haley came home one spring afternoon with two Rhode Island Red baby chickens, I thought to myself, I will get some great Easter photos this year. We figured it would be a learning experience for Haley to raise them.

She started a journal about them, named them Sweetie and Sweetie Pie and, of course, vowed to clean up after them. We knew that eventually they would grow big enough to be ready for farm life, so we arranged a place for them to go after they grew up enough to be on their own.

When Easter weekend got close, I realized the chicks had grown much too fast to still be cute in photos, so what was our solution? That's right, we went out and bought two more. This time we got Foghorn Whites and Tom and I named them Jelly and Bean. They were cute for about two weeks, but not too long after these photos were taken, they got just as gawky and strange looking as the other two.

It turned out to be a great experience, but by the time they got to move to the farm, we were all happy to see them go.

TITLE

PHOTO   PHOTO   PHOTO   PHOTO

PHOTO   PHOTO

PHOTO   JOURNALING

TOY OR FOOD?

Gizmo spent a great deal of time contemplating whether the apple was a toy or food. He thought it was a toy but each time he picked it up his taste buds told him otherwise. After a long stare down, he made the determination that indeed it was food and took a great big bite.

Graphic

Jodi uses an offset piece of vibrant cardstock to mount her photos and journaling, creating a blocked look as opposed to the free-floating look of the sketch. Circle accents are cut from square patterned paper and are mounted along with black cardstock to stay with a graphic feel but add visual variety.

TOY OR FOOD?
Jodi Heinen, Sartell, Minnesota

Supplies: Patterned paper (Arctic Frog); textured cardstocks (Bazzill); letter sticker (American Crafts); paw print punch, circle punches (EK Success)

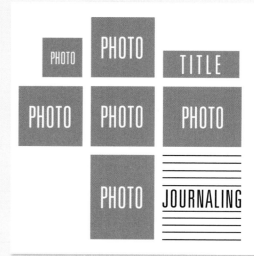

Simple

This sketch's concept provided Kelli with freedom to use a number of photos covering one event and add some accents for interest. To add color around the edges, a strip of patterned paper is layered onto white cardstock and then onto the page. Her title and journaling placement stays true to the sketch, completing her layout.

FLYING
Kelli Noto, Centennial, Colorado

Supplies: Patterned paper, metal letters (Pressed Petals); die-cut snowflakes (QuicKutz); glitter glue (Ranger); cardstock

Enhanced

To carry out her theme but stay with the sketch's photo, title and journaling placement, Lisa uses layers of embellishments to create depth and visual excitement. The guitar strings are angled toward the focal photo, drawing your eye to it. She layers some of the background embellishments onto some of the photos, giving this enhanced layout lots of dimension.

GUITAR GIRL
Lisa Dixon, East Brunswick, New Jersey

Supplies: Patterned paper (Autumn Leaves); textured cardstock (Bazzill); screw eyelets, metal, brads, snaps (Making Memories); extra thick embossing powder (Suze Weinberg); hook and eye fasteners (Prym-Dritz); dimensional adhesive (JudiKins); cord (Yasutomo & Co.); transparency; vellum; stamping ink; basswood; guitar pick, guitar strings; acrylic scraps

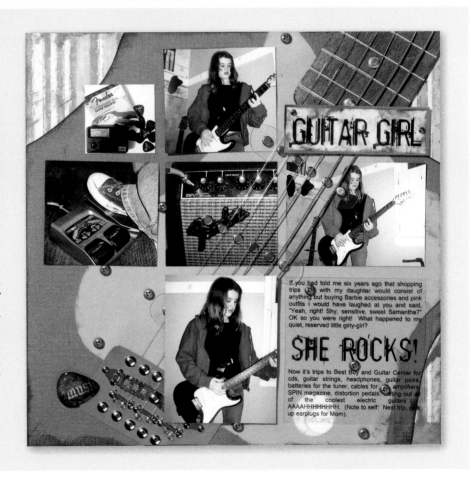

Graphic

To add visual variety to the graphic feel of the sketch, Ronnie alters the title and journaling box on her digital layout to suit her artistic style. Narrowing the journaling and title boxes allowed her to overlap them onto the photos, drawing your eye down and around the layout. A quote is added atop the center photo to enhance it along with a faded clock stamp element, once again drawing your eye through the layout.

THE NAVIGATOR
Ronnie McCray, St. James, Missouri

Supplies: Image-editing software (Adobe Photoshop Elements 2.0); clock stamp (www.cbdigitaldesigns.com)

Simple

Pamela uses vibrant, well-composed photos to get the most from this sketch's design concept. The title is expanded slightly and mounted offset and onto the photo, drawing your eye into the layout. Pamela uses a thin green line around the edge of the layout as yet another way to entice your eye around the various elements.

VIBRANT VERMILION
Pamela James, Ventura, California

Supplies: Textured cardstock (Bazzill, K & Company); die-cut letter stencils (Wishblade); transparency; eyelets

Enhanced

Laurel creates a fantastic display of her travel photos by embracing the sketch's concept of maximizing the space for photos. A colorful backdrop provides interest for the multiple photos that stayed true to the sketch's placement. Laurel creates movement through the page by breaking up her title and placing it in two different spots on the layout, altering the sketch's title placement slightly.

CHICAGO
Laurel Gervitz, Maple Grove, Minnesota

Supplies: Patterned papers (KI Memories); bottle caps (Li'l Davis Designs); flowers, fibers, ribbon (DMD); wooden letters (Walnut Hollow); tag letters (Lara's Crafts); letter stamps (Making Memories); cardstock; ribbon; cording; stamping ink

Graphic

MaryAnn adheres to this sketch's placement concept for her digital layout, making only slight changes to fit her needs and add interest. To suit the size of her photos, the entire page is utilized for them as opposed to the sketch's placement. The top photo is a panoramic sliced into three sections for interest. The bottom photos balance it out by enlarging them to fit across the span of the page, mimicking the panoramic above. For variety the title is placed on the top photo and the journaling expands to tie in to the remainder of the page.

VENTURA COUNTY LINE
MaryAnn Wise, The Woodlands, Texas

Supplies: Image-editing software (Adobe Photoshop CS); ribbon (www.shabbyprincess.com)

Simple

Courtney alters the sketch to suit her unique style with colorful strips of cardstock mounted casually under her title and journaling, causing the two to flow together. Using a zipper accent on the title creates movement into the page. She finishes her layout with small dates affixed on each photo to create a timeline.

UNDENIABLY YOU
Courtney Walsh, Winnebago, Illinois

Supplies: Textured cardstocks (Bazzill); zipper (Junkitz); chipboard letters (Li'l Davis Designs); label maker (Dymo); ribbon (May Arts); stamping ink

Enhanced

Samantha breaks up the uniformity of the sketch and personalizes it to put emphasis on her main photos by enlarging them and framing the focal photo with a boyish embellished frame. The smaller photos on the top of the sketch become supporting photos and are highlighted in a filmstrip overlay. Samantha shortens the length of the title and journaling to leave room for her embellishments, completing her page.

MY SON THE CAPTAIN
Samantha Walker,
Battle Ground, Washington

Supplies: Patterned cardstocks, washer words (Making Memories); photo corners, filmstrip transparency (Creative Imaginations); woven label (Me & My Big Ideas); blue chains (Li'l Davis Designs); coated linen thread (Scrapworks); letter stamps (La Pluma); embossing powder; eyelets; wood ring; brads

Graphic

Diana uses the sketch concept to create a colorful photomontage. Using larger photos than indicated on the sketch and mounting them stacked gives the illusion of a panoramic photo. To draw your eye around the photos, a color-coordinating border is added at the top and bottom of the page.

VIA ARTÉ
Diana Hudson, Bakersfield, California

Supplies: Patterned papers (Scenic Route Paper Co.); rub-on letters (Wordsworth)

Simple

Heidi blocks her background to co-ordinate with the blocked look of the sketch then softens it with fibers and accents. For emphasis on her focal photo, colored photo corners are added. Heidi creates a visual triangle, made with bottle cap embellishments, to draw your eye through the layout and back to the focal photo.

AUNTIE TESSA
Heidi Dillon, Salt Lake City, Utah

Supplies: Patterned paper (KI Memories); textured card-stock, bottle cap embellishments (Club Scrap); die-cut letters (Sizzix); photo corners (Gary M. Burlin & Co.); dimensional adhesive (Ranger); fibers (Timeless Touches); corner rounder (Creative Memories); stamping ink

Enhanced

Jenn tells the story of her son's fondness of baseball through the sketch's concept of maximizing space for photos. The photo sizes were changed from the sketch slightly to add space for the expanded title. To enhance her layout, she sands and paints the edges of her photos and page. Stamped embellishments over-lapped on the photos tie in with her chip-board title to complete her layout.

TEAM PLAYER
Jenn Brookover, San Antonio, Texas

Supplies: Patterned papers (American Traditional Designs, Basic Grey, Daisy D's); stampboard embellishments (Ampersand Art Supply); letter stamps (FontWerks); rub-on letters (Making Memories); chipboard letters (Li'l Davis Designs); rivets (Chatterbox); ribbon (Offray); stamping ink; acrylic paint

Graphic

April creates a digital layout based on this sketch's linear collage concept. The photos, journaling and title box are made larger to cover the entire layout space, varying slightly from the sketch. She uses photos with a variety of colors and transparency depths to give visual interest.

PAUL & KRISTEN
April Anderton, Springville, Utah

Supplies: Image-editing software (Adobe Photoshop CS); digital backgrounds and brushes (www.digitalscrapbooking.com);

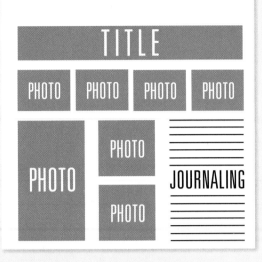

Simple

Colleen chooses both black-and-white and color photos for this sketch, providing visual impact for her layout. To make her focal photo stand out, she double mats it in blue and black cardstocks to coordinate with her patterned paper background. The color photos across the top of the page are stitched around to help set them off from the black-and-white photos. Some color is added to the black-and-white photos with blue brads, tying it into the rest of the page.

COTTESLOE BEACH
Colleen Macdonald, Winthrop, West Australia, Australia

Supplies: Patterned paper, pre-stitched leather strips, rub-on letters, stencil letters (Lil' Davis Designs); mini brads (Provo Craft); cardstock; stamping ink

Enhanced

Torrey utilizes the sketch to tell a story with her photos and enhances it with many dimensional embellishments. To create a visual division of the layout, a chain is used to divide it into thirds. The smaller supporting photos are attached to it with picture hangers surrounding the focal photo. She expands the title to balance out the photos and pops it to coordinate with the dimension of the remainder page. For visual interest, the journaling and title are matted on a stitched piece of fabric.

N SINK
Torrey Scott, Thornton, Colorado

Supplies: Patterned vellum (PrintWorks); letter stencils (Making Memories); epoxy letters (Creative Imaginations); cat sticker (Jo-Ann Stores); dimensional paint (Plaid); watermark ink (Tsukineko); paw-print stamp (Inkadinkado); polymer clay (Eberhard Faber); cardstock; ball chain; picture hangers; brads; acrylic paint

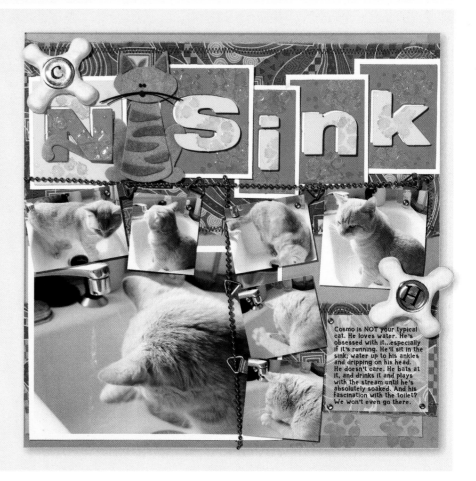

Graphic

Danielle uses the graphic feel of the sketch for photo placement, modifying it by using different colored and sized photos. Photos of her sunflower mural provide the color scheme for the layout, which is re-enforced in her photos that are altered before printing. Danielle chooses to mount her photos stacked and put her title and journaling together for continuity, altering the sketch slightly.

MY LITTLE SUNFLOWER
Danielle Thompson, Tucker, Georgia

Supplies: Patterned paper (Creative Imaginations); flower sticker (Pressed Petals); cardstock; transparency

Simple

Holle shares a year in her husband's and her life season by season thanks to the model of this sketch. To unify and harmonize the photo placement on both sides of her page, she uses striped patterned paper on the background. The title is tied in to the journaling by matting both together on the page as opposed to each having its own space as shown on the sketch.

COLORADO LIVING
Holle Wiktorek, Reunion, Colorado

Supplies: Patterned paper (Pressed Petals); letter stamps (La Pluma); cardstock; stamping ink

As Tennessee natives, Thomas and I had a lot to learn when we moved to Colorado. The altitude was a challenge to face, and the experience of four seasons in one day was new to us. Although Thomas and I aren't skiers, we enjoy the snow and the mountain's majesty. We miss the Tennessee trees, but we enjoy the beautiful view seen for miles. The amazing sunrises and sunsets remind us of God's daily hand in our lives, and finding Trinity United Methodist Church in downtown Denver makes our Colorado journey more complete. We spend holidays without our entire family, but our friendly neighborhood helps us make new memories. While in Colorado, Thomas works at Buckley Air Force Base and I work in my home studio. The Army won't keep us living in Colorado for long, so we look for the positive in our western adventure.

Enhanced

Jennifer enhances this sketch to make room for extra embellishments, creating a feminine page that is unique to her. The photos on the left are moved down and mounted on a single stitched section, leaving room for her accents. To draw your eye down on the page, Jennifer creates a title and journaling box combination overlapping the letters onto her main photos. To tie her page together, a similar accent is added on the journaling box.

MAKE A WISH
Jennifer S. Gallacher, Savannah, Georgia

Supplies: Patterned papers (C-Thru Ruler, Karen Foster Design, Making Memories); textured cardstock (Bazzill); pearl buckles, rub-on word (Li'l Davis Designs); alphabet and patterned tags, large letters (C-Thru Ruler); letter stamps (PSX Design); metal word charm (Karen Foster Design); beads (Willow Bead); silk flowers; tulle; safety pins; ribbon; stamping ink; transparency; brads

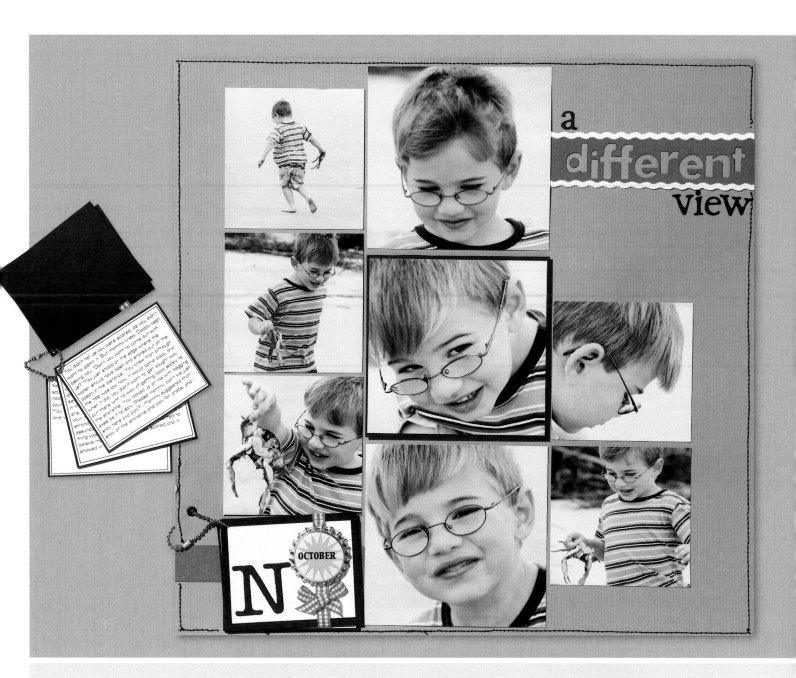

Graphic

Holly keeps with the sketch's placement of elements but uses a storybook type of journaling idea to tell her complete tale behind the photos. The book is hung on a key chain for easy opening and embellished on the cover for visual interest. To draw your eye to the title and around the photos, a red strip of cardstock is used for the title cutout. A red strip is then mounted on the opposite corner of the page to vaguely reflect the cut title and draw your eye through the layout.

A DIFFERENT VIEW
Holly Corbett, Central, South Carolina

Supplies: Textured cardstock (Bazzill); die-cut letters (QuicKutz); bottle cap embellishment, rub-on word (Li'l Davis Designs); ribbon, rickrack (Making Memories); cardstock

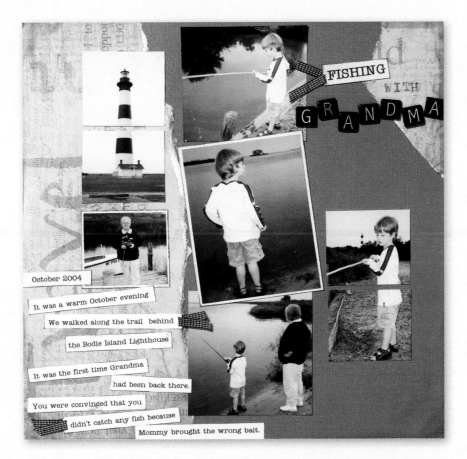

Simple

Dana creatively alters her photos in order to stay with the sketch's placement but fit her own needs. The smaller supporting photos are actually single photos cut into sections and mounted around the larger focal photos. She draws attention to the focal photo by matting it and adhering it offset. To vary her title from the sketch, Dana uses strip-style journaling as opposed to the title box on the sketch.

FISHING WITH GRANDMA
Dana Swords, Doswell, Virginia

Supplies: Patterned paper (Daisy D's); textured cardstock (Bazzill); letter stamps (EK Success); letter tiles (DMD); ribbon (Offray); stamping ink

Enhanced

Suzy uses the sketch's many photos to capture her daughter's various faces in a photo-shoot-type setting. For a unique twist on her main photo, Suzy mats it atop an enlarged version and adds metal photo corners. Index prints are added to the supporting photos as accents and for visual variety. The title and journaling tag are tied together with matching ribbons.

BELIEVE IN YOURSELF
Suzy West, Fremont, California

Supplies: Patterned paper, rub-on words (Imagination Project); metal photo corners (source unknown); ribbons (May Arts); canvas tags (source unknown); transparency

Graphic

Michelle uses lines to break up the very graphic look of the sketch and give her digital layout a subtle cross design. For a more dramatic feel, the photos are matted on white and placed on a black background. To complete her layout, she adds a graphic accent at the top, enhancing her title.

ETERNAL LOVE
Michelle Shefveland, Sauk Rapids, Minnesota

Supplies: Image-editing software (Adobe Photoshop Elements 3.0); digital background, diamond border, swirled wooden mat, and copper brads (CottageArts.net)

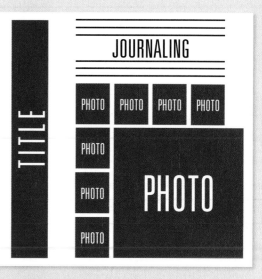

eternal

scott and lisa, your love story is one of true miracles. my prayer for you is that you always hold on to the precious realization that god brought you together in the most amazing of ways, and that he has a purpose for your eternal love that will change the world.

aug.07.04

Simple

Holly makes use of the sketch's placement of supporting photos to call attention to the focal photo by printing them in black-and-white. Simple variations to the sketch are made such as rounding the corners of the title and journaling box, and adding accents to them such as ribbon and die-cut flowers for her own style and flair.

PRINCESS TEA PARTY
Holly VanDyne, Mansfield, Ohio

Supplies: Patterned paper, letter stickers, patterned tag (Basic Grey); die-cut flowers (QuicKutz); ribbon (Michaels); brads (Making Memories); cardstock; acrylic paint

Enhanced

Angie shows her personal style on this sketch using a variety of ribbons accenting a photo box, and her hand-cut title that duplicates the Memory Makers Masters logo. A gingham ribbon highlights the focal photo while paper flowers with ribbon bow centers achieve the same look on the journaling box, completing the layout.

MEMORY MAKERS MASTERS
Angie Head, Friendswood, Texas

Supplies: Textured cardstocks (Prism Papers); ribbons (Bobbin Ribbon, Making Memories, Offray); paper flowers (Prima); brads

Reproducible Sketches

Here you'll find all of the six- or more photo sketches used in Chapter 4. Use these handy reproducible sketches to complete your own unique scrapbook pages, altering the sketch a tiny bit to fit your personal style or rotating the sketch to fit your layout needs. Simply photocopy the sketches, enlarging if desired to fit your sketch organizational system.

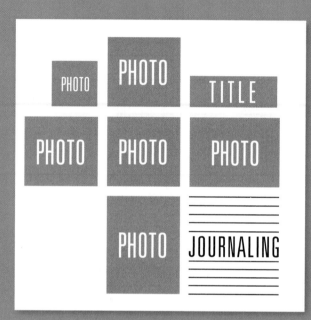

- PAGE **74** -

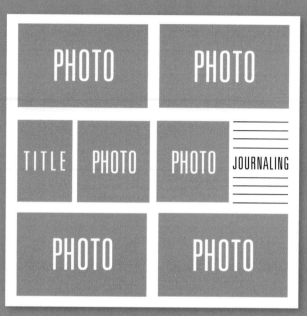

- PAGE **76** -

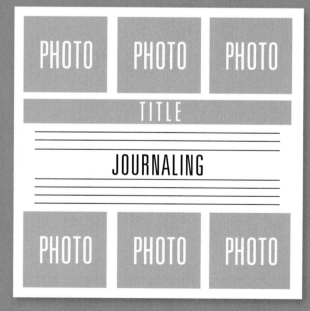

- PAGE **78** -

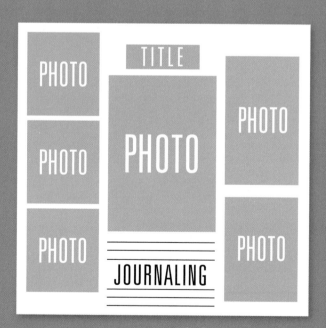

- PAGE **80** -

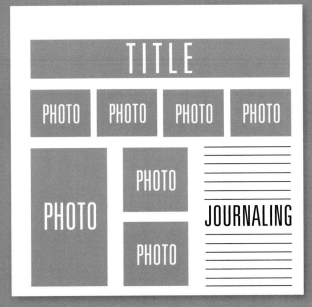

- PAGE **82** -

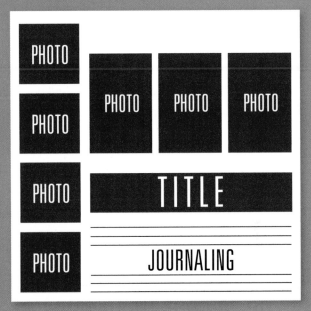

- PAGE **84** -

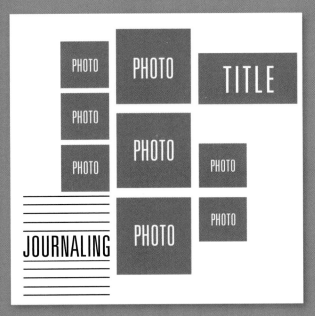

- PAGE **86** -

- PAGE **88** -

Additional Instructions & Credits

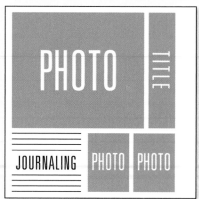

Cover art
COMMUTE
Jodi cleverly slides all elements shown on the sketch over to left of the page to allow room for her graphic "clock" elements to denote a typical work day.

Jodi Amidei, Memory Makers Books

Photos: Nick Nyffeler, Memory Makers Books; Ken Trujillo, Memory Makers

Supplies: Patterned paper (SEI); corner rounder punches (EK Success); square punches (EK Success, Family Treasures); die-cut letters (QuicKutz)

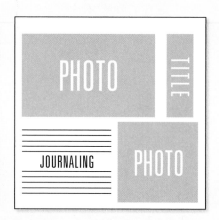

Page 4
THE GREAT GUMBALL HUNTER
Jodi follows the sketch precisely, with the exception of the photo corners touching, to create a tantalizing layout.

Jodi Amidei, Memory Makers Books

Photos: MaryJo Regier, Memory Makers Books

Supplies: Circle punch, corner rounder punch (EK Success); image-editing software (Adobe); cardstock

Page 6
PLEASE DADDY
Jodi uses the same sketch to create a two-page spread by simply rotating the sketch for the right-hand page.

Jodi Amidei, Memory Makers Books

Supplies: Patterned paper (KI Memories, Scrappy Cat); mini brads (Making Memories); corner rounder punches (EK Success, Punch Bunch); handcut title

Page 9
KEEPING SKETCHES ORGANIZED
All created by Jodi Amidei, Memory Makers Books

Supplies: Notebook: Spiral notebook (DMD); patterned paper (Carolee's Creations); die-cut letters (QuicKutz); ribbon (May Arts); cardstock; pen. Mini Index File Folder: Patterned paper (Carolee's Creations); letter stickers (Creative Imaginations); index file folder; cardstock; pen. Index File Box: Letter stickers, floral stickers (Creative Imaginations); index box; cardstock; pen. Binder: Cardstock; binder; pen; tab dividers

Page 10

HEARTBREAKER IN TRAINING

Jodi adapts the sketch a little by trimming the photo smaller than shown in the sketch to accommodate a large graphic element of patterned paper on her page.

Jodi Amidei, Memory Makers Books

Photo: Emily Cooley, Broomfield, Colorado

Supplies: Patterned paper (KI Memories); textured cardstocks (Canson, Prism Papers); die-cut letters (QuicKutz); handcut title

Page 28

DANIELLE

Jodi turns the focal photo vertically, a slight variation from the sketch, to allow more room for her graphic border.

Jodi Amidei, Memory Makers Books

Supplies: Textured cardstocks (Bazzill, Prism Papers); patterned vellum (source unknown); circle cutter (Creative Memories); corner rounder punch (EK Success); clear embossing powder; handcut title

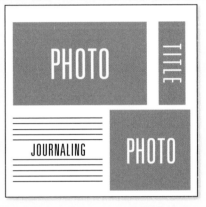

Page 50

PILING ON

Jodi softens the sketch layout with rounded photo corners and playful patterned papers and title treatment.

Jodi Amidei, Memory Makers Books

Supplies: Patterned paper (KI Memories); flower charms (Making Memories); corner rounder punch (EK Success); circle cutter (Creative Memories); handcut title

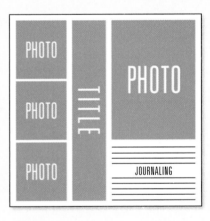

Page 72

CHICKS

Jodi cleverly alters the sketch a tiny bit to be able to corral stacked images inside a graphic background design of punched circles.

Jodi Amidei, Memory Makers Books

Photos: Kelli Noto, Centennial, Colorado

Supplies: Textured cardstock (Canson, Prism Papers); circle punch (Fiskars); corner rounder punch (EK Success); handcut title

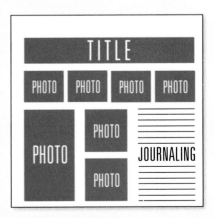

Source Guide

The following companies manufacture products featured in this book. Please check your local retailers to find these materials, or go to a company's Web site for the latest product. In addition, we have made every attempt to properly credit the items mentioned in this book. We apologize to any company that we have listed incorrectly, and we would appreciate hearing from you.

2DYE4
www.canscrapink.com

7 Gypsies
(800) 588-6707
www.7gypsies.com

Accu-Cut®
(800) 288-1670
www.accucut.com

Adobe Systems Incorporated
(866) 766-2256
www.adobe.com

Alien Skin Software, LLC
(888) 921-SKIN
www.alienskin.com

All My Memories
(888) 553-1998
www.allmymemories.com

All Night Media
(see Plaid Enterprises)

American Art Clay Co. (AMACO)
(800) 374-1600
www.amaco.com

American Crafts
(801) 226-0747
www.americancrafts.com

American Traditional Designs®
(800) 448-6656
www.americantraditional.com

Ampersand Art Supply
(800) 822-1939
www.ampersandart.com

Anna Griffin, Inc.
(888) 817-8170
www.annagriffin.com

Arctic Frog
(479) 636-FROG
www.arcticfrog.com

Autumn Leaves
(800) 588-6707
www.autumnleaves.com

Avery Dennison Corporation
(800) GO-AVERY
www.avery.com

Basic Grey™
(801) 451-6006
www.basicgrey.com

Bazzill Basics Paper
(480) 558-8557
www.bazzillbasics.com

Beads & Plenty More
(517) 47-BEADS
www.beadsandplentymore.com

Bella Press
(253) 437-1626
www.bellapress.com

Blue Moon Beads
(800) 377-6715
www.bluemoonbeads.com

Bobbin Ribbon- no contact info

Boutique Trims, Inc.
(248) 437-2017
www.boutiquetrims.com

Boxer Scrapbook Productions
(503) 625-0455
www.boxerscrapbooks.com

Bull Dog- no contact info

Canson®, Inc.
(800) 628-9283
www.canson-us.com

Card Connection- see Michaels

CARL Mfg. USA, Inc.
(800) 257-4771
www.Carl-Products.com

Carolee's Creations®
(435) 563-1100
www.ccpaper.com

Chatterbox, Inc.
(208) 939-9133
www.chatterboxinc.com

Clearsnap, Inc.
(360) 293-6634
www.clearsnap.com

Cloud 9 Design
(763) 493-0990
www.cloud9design.biz

Club Scrap™, Inc.
(888) 634-9100
www.clubscrap.com

Collections- no contact info

Colorbök™, Inc.
(800) 366-4660
www.colorbok.com

CottageArts.net™
www.cottagearts.net

Crafts, Etc. Ltd.
(800) 888-0321
www.craftsetc.com

Creative Imaginations
(800) 942-6487
www.cigift.com

Creative Memories®
(800) 468-9335
www.creativememories.com

Creek Bank Creations, Inc.
(217) 427-5980
www.creekbankcreations.com

C-Thru® Ruler Company, The
(800) 243-8419
www.cthruruler.com

Current®, Inc.
(800) 848-2848
www.currentinc.com

Daisy D's Paper Company
(888) 601-8955
www.daisydspaper.com

Design Originals
(800) 877-0067
www.d-originals.com

Designs by Reminisce
(319) 358-9777
www.shopreminisce.com

DieCuts with a View™
(877) 221-6107
www.dcwv.com

DMD Industries, Inc.
(800) 805-9890
www.dmdind.com

Doodlebug Design™ Inc.
(801) 966-9952
www.doodlebug.ws

Dymo
www.dymo.com

Eberhard Faber
www.eberhardfaber.de

Eco-Africa-USA, Inc.
(888) 779-7077
www.naturallypaper.com

EK Success™, Ltd.
(800) 524-1349
www.eksuccess.com

Europa Imports, Inc.
(800) 778-0717
www.europatrimmings.com

Family Treasures, Inc.®
www.familytreasures.com

Fiskars®, Inc.
(800) 950-0203
www.fiskars.com

FontWerks
(604) 942-3105
www.fontwerks.com

Gary M. Burlin & Co.
(800) 659-PENS
www.garymburlin.com

Gauchogirl Creative
www.gauchogirl.com

Go West Studios
(214) 227-0007
www.goweststudios.com

Graphic Products Corporation
(800) 323-1658
www.gpcpapers.com

Halcraft USA
(212) 376-1580
www.halcraft.com

Heidi Swapp/Advantus Corporation
(904) 482-0092
www.heidiswapp.com

Hero Arts® Rubber Stamps, Inc.
(800) 822-4376
www.heroarts.com

Hirschberg Schutz & Co., Inc.
(800) 221-8640

Hot Off The Press, Inc.
(800) 227-9595
www.paperpizazz.com

HyGlo®/American Pin
(480) 968-6475
www.hyglocrafts.com

Imagination Project, Inc.
(513) 860-2711
www.imaginationproject.com

Inkadinkado® Rubber Stamps
(800) 888-4652
www.inkadinkado.com

Ink It- no contact info

Jaquard Products/Rupert, Gibbon & Spider, Inc.
(800) 442-0455
www.jacquardproducts.com

Jest Charming
(702) 564-5101
www.jestcharming.com

JewelCraft, LLC
(201) 223-0804
www.jewelcraft.biz

Jo-Ann Stores
(888) 739-4120
www.joann.com

JudiKins
(310) 515-1115
www.judikins.com

Junkitz™
(732) 792-1108
www.junkitz.com

K & Company
(888) 244-2083
www.kandcompany.com
Karen Foster Design
(801) 451-9779
www.karenfosterdesign.com
Keepsake Miniatures- no contact info
KI Memories
(972) 243-5595
www.kimemories.com
Kopp Design
(801) 489-6011
www.koppdesign.com
Krylon®
(216) 566-200
www.krylon.com
La Pluma, Inc.
(803) 749-4076
www.debrabeagle.com
Lara's Crafts
(800) 232-5272
www.larascrafts.com
Lasting Impressions for Paper, Inc.
(801) 298-1979
www.lastingimpressions.com
Leave Memories
www.leavememories.com
Li'l Davis Designs
(949) 838-0344
www.lildavisdesigns.com
Lincraft
www.lincraft.com.au
Magenta Rubber Stamps
(800) 565-5254
www.magentastyle.com
Magic Mesh
(651) 345-6374
www.magicmesh.com
Making Memories
(800) 286-5263
www.makingmemories.com
Ma Vinci's Reliquary
http://crafts.dm.net/mall/reliquary/
May Arts
(800) 442-3950
www.mayarts.com
McGill, Inc.
(800) 982-9884
www.mcgillinc.com
me & my BiG ideas®
(949) 883-2065
www.meandmybigideas.com
Melissa Frances/Heart & Home, Inc.
(905) 686-9031
www.melissafrances.com
Memories Complete™, LLC
(866) 966-6365
www.memoriescomplete.com
Memories in the Making/Leisure Arts
(800) 643-8030
www.leisurearts.com
Michaels® Arts & Crafts
(800) 642-4235
www.michaels.com
Microsoft Corporation
www.microsoft.com
Mrs. Grossman's Paper Company
(800) 429-4549
www.mrsgrossmans.com
Mustard Moon™
(408) 299-8542
www.mustardmoon.com
My Mind's Eye™, Inc.
(800) 665-5116
www.frame-ups.com
Nunn Design
(360) 379-3557
www.nunndesign.com

Offray
www.offray.com
Paper Adventures®
(800) 525-3196
www.paperadventures.com
Paper Company, The/ANW Crestwood
(800) 525-3196
www.anwcrestwood.com
Paper Fever, Inc.
(800) 477-0902
www.paperfever.com
Paper Loft
(866) 254-1961
www.paperloft.com
Pebbles Inc.
(801) 224-1857
www.pebblesinc.com
Plaid Enterprises, Inc.
(800) 842-4197
www.plaidonline.com
PM designs
(888) 595-2887
www.designsbypm.com
Polyform Products Co.
(847) 427-0020
www.sculpey.com
Pressed Petals
(800) 748-4656
www.pressedpetals.com
Prima
(909) 627-5532
www.mulberrypaperflowers.com
PrintWorks
(800) 854-6558
www.printworks.com
Prism™ Papers
(866) 902-1002
www.prismpapers.com
Provo Craft®
(888) 577-3545
www.provocraft.com
Prym-Dritz Corporation
www.dritz.com
PSX Design™
(800) 782-6748
www.psxdesign.com
Punch Bunch, The
(254) 791-4209
www.thepunchbunch.com
QuicKutz
(801) 765-1144
www.quickutz.com
QVC®
www.qvc.com
Ranger Industries, Inc.
(800) 244-2211
www.rangerink.com
Rusty Pickle
(801) 746-1045
www.rustypickle.com
Sandylion Sticker Designs
(800) 387-4215
www.sandylion.com
Sanford® Corporation
(800) 323-0749
www.sanfordcorp.com
Sarah Heidt Photo Craft, LLC
(734) 424-2776
www.sarahheidtphotocraft.com
Scenic Route Paper Co.
(801) 785-0761
www.scenicroutepaper.com
ScrapGoods™ (a division of The Scrap Pack)
www.scrapgoods.com
Scrappy Cat™, LLC
(440) 234-4850
www.scrappycatcreations.com

Scraptivity™ Scrapbooking, Inc.
(800) 393-2151
www.scraptivity.com
Scrapworks, LLC
(801) 363-1010
www.scrapworks.com
SEI, Inc.
(800) 333-3279
www.shopsei.com
Sizzix®
(866) 742-4447
www.sizzix.com
Stamp Craf- see Plaid Enterprises
Stampabilities®
(800) 888-0321
www.stampabilities.com
Sticker Studio™
(208) 322-2465
www.stickerstudio.com
Strano Designs
(508) 454-4615
www.stranodesigns.com
Suze Weinberg Design Studio
(732) 761-2400
www.schmoozewithsuze.com
Timeless Touches™/Dove Valley Productions, LLC
(623) 362-8285
www.timelesstouches.net
Tsukineko®, Inc.
(800) 769-6633
www.tsukineko.com
USArtQuest, Inc.
(517) 522-6225
www.usartquest.com
Wal-Mart Stores, Inc.
(800) WALMART
www.walmart.com
Walnut Hollow® Farm, Inc.
(800) 950-5101
www.walnuthollow.com
Westrim® Crafts
(800) 727-2727
www.westrimcrafts.com
Willow Bead
(866) 488-2323
www.willowbead.com
Wishblade™, Inc.
(651) 644-5144
www.wishblade.com
Wordsworth
(719) 282-3495
www.wordsworthstamps.com
Wübie Prints
(888) 256-0107
www.wubieprints.com
Yasutomo and Company
(650) 737-8888
www.yasutomo.com

Index